Quotable
Men
of the
Twentieth
Century

QUOTABLE

MEN

OF THE

TWENTIETH

CENTURY

Edited by Jessica Allen

WILLIAM MORROW AND COMPANY, INC. / NEW YORK

Library of Congress Cataloging-in-Publication Data has been applied for.
ISBN 0-688-16285-1

Printed in the United States of America

First Edition

1   2   3   4   5   6   7   8   9   10

BOOK DESIGN BY JO ANNE METSCH

www.williammorrow.com

To my brother

Life itself is a quotation.
—JORGE LUIS BORGES

Contents

Acknowledgments

Professionally, I would like to sincerely thank Bill Adler, Jr., for believing in me and for giving me this opportunity, and Tracy Quinn, for her advice, technical support, and jokes.

On a personal note, I must mention those whose presence in my life has created a web that catches me when I fall and bounces me back to success: Sandra D., for the lessons; Lori, for listening; Yos, for the smiles; Eddie and Joyce, for loving me; Sara, for sharing; Joy, for her support; Ingrid, for understanding; Ken, for the laughter; Phil, for being there, always and without question; and Jake, for saving me. I hope that the respect, loyalty, admiration, and love I have for each of you annul the debt I owe you all.

QUOTABLE
MEN
OF THE
TWENTIETH
CENTURY

Achievement

My mother is my root foundation. She planted the seed that I base my life on, and that is the belief that the ability to achieve starts in your mind.

MICHAEL JORDAN

Those who dare to fail miserably can achieve greatly.

ROBERT F. KENNEDY

Man, unlike any other thing organic or inorganic in the universe, grows beyond his work, walks up the stairs of his concepts, emerges ahead of his accomplishments.

JOHN STEINBECK

The higher a monkey climbs, the more you see of its behind.

JOSEPH STILWELL

The achievements of which society rewards are won at the cost of diminution of personality.

CARL JUNG

Any jackass can kick down a barn, but it takes a good carpenter to build one.

SAM RAYBURN

It is sobering to consider that when Mozart was my age he had already been dead for a year.

TOM LEHRER

If I had done everything I'm credited with, I'd be speaking to you from a laboratory jar at Harvard.

FRANK SINATRA

Acting

My dear boy, forget about the motivation. Just say the lines and don't trip over the furniture.

NOEL COWARD

Do your job and demand your compensation—but in that order.

CARY GRANT

Acting is a masochistic form of exhibitionism. It is not quite the occupation of an adult.

LAURENCE OLIVIER

I can't act. I can't ride. I can't sing. And I've got millions of dollars to prove it.

GENE AUTRY

A lot of what acting is is paying attention.

ROBERT REDFORD

I felt that some of the Western stars of the twenties and thirties were too perfect. I made up my mind I was going to play a *real* man.

JOHN WAYNE

I find it rather easy to portray a businessman. Being bland, rather cruel, and incompetent comes naturally to me.

JOHN CLEESE

Acting is about honesty. If you can fake that, you've got it made.

GEORGE BURNS

Maybe being an introvert gives me, by sheer accident, a certain screen presence, a mystique.

CLINT EASTWOOD

Activism

Inaction may be the highest form of action.

JERRY BROWN

You're either part of the solution or part of the problem.
ELDRIDGE CLEAVER

It is easier to fight for one's principles than to live up to them.
ALFRED ADLER

As long as the world shall last there will be wrongs, and if no man objected and no man rebelled, those wrongs would last forever.
CLARENCE S. DARROW

I wear a suit when I'm arrested. I think it helps to remind people that this isn't a rowdy act but a carefully considered demonstration that I deem worthy of great respect.
BENJAMIN SPOCK

Organize the unorganized.
JOHN LLEWELLYN LEWIS

I have cherished the ideal of a democratic and free society in which all persons live together in harmony with equal opportunities. It is an ideal which I hope to live for and see realized. But, if needs be, it is an ideal for which I am prepared to die.
NELSON MANDELA

There is a giant asleep within every man. When that giant wakes, miracles happen.

MAX BRAND

Through my years of challenging a host of injustices, I have learned that those in power regard every act of protest—whether against the most mundane rule or the most fundamental principle—as equally threatening.

DERRICK BELL

Every revolutionary ends up by becoming either an oppressor or a heretic.

ALBERT CAMUS

If you will protest courageously, and yet with dignity and Christian love, when the history books are written in future generations the historians will have to pause and say, "There lived a great people—a black people—who injected new meaning and dignity into the veins of civilization."

MARTIN LUTHER KING, JR.

Things do not happen. They are made to happen.

JOHN F. KENNEDY

You can't fight for just one group of oppressed people and hate another. It is just inconceivable.

AL SHARPTON

America I'm putting my queer shoulder to the wheel.

ALLEN GINSBERG

I believe in the doctrine of non-violence as a weapon of the weak. I believe in the doctrine of non-violence as a weapon of the strongest. I believe that a man is the strongest soldier for daring to die unarmed.

MAHATMA GANDHI

If any demonstrator ever lays down in front of my car, it'll be the last car he'll ever lay down in front of.

GEORGE C. WALLACE

Actors

Every actor in his heart believes every bad thing that's printed about him.

ORSON WELLES

I have to act to live.

LAURENCE OLIVIER

I never drank nor smoked in a picture. Kids came to see my pictures. I didn't think it was right for them to see drinking or smoking on screen.

KEN MAYNARD

I enjoy being a highly overpaid actor.

ROGER MOORE

If an actor has a message, he should call Western Union. An actor's job is to act, nothing more.

HUMPHREY BOGART

I never said all actors are cattle. What I said was all actors should be *treated* like cattle.

ALFRED HITCHCOCK

The movie actor, like the sacred king of primitive tribes, is a god in captivity.

ALEXANDER CHASE

An actor's a guy who, if you ain't talking about him, ain't listening.

MARLON BRANDO

I'm notorious for giving a bad interview. I'm an actor and I can't help but feel I'm boring when I'm myself.

ROCK HUDSON

ADVICE

I realize that advice is worth what it costs—nothing.

DOUGLAS MACARTHUR

1. Avoid fried meats which angry up the blood. 2. If your stomach disputes you, lie down and pacify it with cool thoughts. 3. Keep the juices flowing by jangling around gently as you move. 4. Go very lightly on the vices, such as carrying on in society. The social ramble ain't restful. 5. Avoid running at all times. 6. Don't look back. Something might be gaining on you.

SATCHEL PAIGE

Never trust anyone over thirty.

ABBIE HOFFMAN

A word to the wise ain't necessary—it's the stupid ones who need the advice.

BILL COSBY

Always keep your word. A gentleman never insults anyone unintentionally. Don't look for trouble, but if you get into a fight, make sure you win it.

JOHN WAYNE

If you can give your son only one gift, let it be enthusiasm.

BRUCE BARTON

Learn to take your work seriously and not yourself seriously.

CLINT EASTWOOD

Never let the fear of striking out get in your way.

BABE RUTH

The only justification for ever looking down on someone is to pick them up.

JESSE JACKSON

Be kind to cops; they're not cops, they're people in disguise who've been deceived by their own disguise.

ALLEN GINSBERG

Chop your own wood, and it will warm you twice.

HENRY FORD

No one wants advice—only corroboration.

JOHN STEINBECK

Never eat at a place called Mom's. Never play cards with a man named Doc. And never lay down with a woman who's got more troubles than you.

NELSON ALGREN

Don't let your mouth write no check your tail can't cash.

BO DIDDLEY

Act locally, but think globally.

RENÉ DUBOS

Dad gave me two pieces of advice. One was, "No matter how good you think you are, there are people better than you." But he was an optimist too; his other advice: "Never worry about rejection. Every day is a new beginning."

JOHN RITTER

Aging

I ain't what I used to be, but who the hell is?

DIZZY DEAN

Growing old is like being increasingly penalized for a crime you haven't committed.

ANTHONY POWELL

The four stages of man are infancy, childhood, adolescence, and obsolescence.

ART LINKLETTER

Middle age is having a choice of two temptations and choosing the one that will get you home earlier.

DAN BENNETT

I will never be an old man. To me, old age is always fifteen years older than I am.

BERNARD BARUCH

At my age, when a girl flirts with me in the movies, she's after my popcorn.

MILTON BERLE

A man knows when he is growing old because he begins to look like his father.

GABRIEL GARCÍA MÁRQUEZ

You can't help getting older but you don't have to get old.

GEORGE BURNS

Middle age is when you've met so many people that every new person you meet reminds you of someone else.

OGDEN NASH

I don't feel eighty. In fact I don't feel *anything* until noon. Then it's time for my nap.

BOB HOPE

First you forget names; then you forget faces; then you forget to zip up your fly; and then you forget to unzip your fly.

BRANCH RICKEY

Old age has its pleasures, which though different, are not less than the pleasures of youth.

W. SOMERSET MAUGHAM

The years between fifty and seventy are the hardest. You are always being asked to do things, and yet you are not decrepit enough to turn them down.

T. S. ELIOT

Age is a question of mind over matter. If you don't mind, it doesn't matter.

SATCHEL PAIGE

Just remember, once you're over the hill you begin to pick up speed.

CHARLES M. SCHULZ

Old age is the most unexpected of all things that happen to a man.

LEON TROTSKY

I recently turned fifty, which is young for a tree, midlife for an elephant, and ancient for a quarter miler, whose son now says, "Dad, I just can't run the quarter with you anymore unless I bring something to read."

BILL COSBY

Anyone can get old. All you have to do is live long enough.

GROUCHO MARX

I am a child who is getting on.

MARC CHAGALL

Alcohol

I'd hate to be a teetotaler. Imagine getting up in the morning and knowing that's as good as you're going to feel all day.

DEAN MARTIN

First you take a drink, then the drink takes a drink, then the drink takes you.

F. SCOTT FITZGERALD

I have to think hard to name an interesting man who does not drink.

RICHARD BURTON

Actually, it takes one drink to get me loaded. Trouble is, I can't remember if it's the thirteenth or fourteenth.

GEORGE BURNS

I spent ninety percent of my salary on good Irish whiskey and women. The rest I wasted.

TUG MCGRAW

Alcohol is the anesthesia by which we endure the operation of life.

GEORGE BERNARD SHAW

An alcoholic is someone you don't like who drinks as much as you do.

DYLAN THOMAS

Drink the first. Sip the second slowly. Skip the third.

KNUTE ROCKNE

I'm no alcoholic. I'm a drunkard. The difference is drunkards don't go to meetings.

JACKIE GLEASON

I can't look forward to going out and getting drunk on a given night anymore, which I used to love. That was the way to get back to oneself, and I can't do it. Because I wake up in the morning and I can't get out of bed.

NORMAN MAILER

I always wake up at the crack of ice.

JOE LEWIS

I've made it a rule never to drink by daylight and never refuse a drink after dark.

H. L. MENCKEN

I drink to make other people more interesting.

GEORGE JEAN NATHAN

Ambition

Do it big or stay in bed.

LARRY KELLY

You can do anything in this world if you are prepared to take the consequences.

W. SOMERSET MAUGHAM

I intend to be here for the long haul.

SPIKE LEE

Despair is the price one pays for setting oneself an impossible aim.

GRAHAM GREENE

All I want out of life is that when I walk down the street folks will say, "There goes the greatest hitter who ever lived."

TED WILLIAMS

I believe that I was destined to do more than just hit tennis balls.

ARTHUR ASHE

Nothing great will ever be achieved without great men, and men are great only if they are determined to be so.

CHARLES DE GAULLE

I'd like to be rich enough to throw soap away after the letters are worn off.

ANDY ROONEY

I'm not a legend yet. I just work hard at what I do.

SHAQUILLE O'NEAL

Appearance

Ugliness is a point of view. An ulcer is wonderful to a pathologist.

AUSTIN O'MALLEY

Eyes lie if you look into them for the character of a person.

STEVIE WONDER

Gray hair is God's graffiti.

BILL COSBY

Beauty is an ecstasy; it is as simple as hunger. There is really nothing else to be said about it.

W. SOMERSET MAUGHAM

My face looks like a wedding cake that has been left out in the rain.

W. H. AUDEN

Hair that's cut fights back. It rebels. And it always gets the last laugh, continuing to grow even when the rest of you is laid out on the slab.

DON KING

After a degree of prettiness, one girl is as pretty as another.

F. SCOTT FITZGERALD

I never forget a face, but in your case I'll be glad to make an exception.

GROUCHO MARX

Ugliness is a sin.

FRANK LLOYD WRIGHT

It is easy to be beautiful; it is difficult to appear so.

FRANK O'HARA

So I'm ugly. So what? I never saw anyone hit with his face.

YOGI BERRA

Art

All art is based on non-conformity.

BEN SHAHN

Art is the unceasing effort to compete with the beauty of flowers—and never succeeding.

MARC CHAGALL

Treat a work of art like a prince. Let it speak to you first.

ARTHUR SCHOPENHAUER

Art does not reproduce the visible; rather, it makes visible.

PAUL KLEE

Modern art is what happens when painters stop looking at girls and persuade themselves that they have a better idea.

JOHN CIARDI

The subject matter of art is life, life as it actually is; but the function of art is to make life better.

GEORGE SANTAYANA

All art is propaganda . . . On the other hand, not all propaganda is art.

GEORGE ORWELL

The understanding of art depends finally upon one's willingness to extend one's humanity and one's knowledge of human life.

RALPH ELLISON

Beauty plus pity—that is the closest we can get to a definition of art.

VLADIMIR NABOKOV

I deeply believe that art has a social responsibility—not only to show how life is, but to show how life should be.

HARRY BELAFONTE

We must never forget that art is not a form of propaganda; it is a form of truth.

JOHN F. KENNEDY

Art is a lie which makes us realize truth.

PABLO PICASSO

Art is cultural insurance. Take out a policy now.

THEO CROSBY

Maybe art cannot always change minds, but art can change hearts.

JAMES EARL JONES

I am for an art that is political-erotical-mystical, that does something other than sit on its ass in a museum.

CLAES OLDENBURG

A great work of art is like a dream; for all its apparent obviousness it does not explain itself and is never unequivocal.

CARL JUNG

Artists

An artist is somebody who produces things people don't need.

ANDY WARHOL

A good artist should be isolated. If he isn't isolated, something is wrong.

ORSON WELLES

The refusal to rest content, the willingness to risk excess on behalf of one's obsessions, is what distinguishes artists from entertainers, and what makes some artists adventurers on behalf of us all.

JOHN UPDIKE

Any artist should be grateful for a naïve grace which puts him beyond the need to reason elaborately.

SAUL BELLOW

Painting is stronger than I am. It can make me do whatever it wants.

PABLO PICASSO

The attitude that nature is chaotic and that the artist puts order into it is a very absurd point of view, I think. All that we can hope for is to put some order into ourselves.

WILLEM DE KOONING

An artist is his own fault.

JOHN O'HARA

The artist must penetrate into the world, feel the fate of human beings, of people, with real love. There is no art for art's sake—one must be interested in the whole realm of life.

MARC CHAGALL

The great artists of the world are never puritans, and seldom even ordinarily respectable.

H. L. MENCKEN

It does not matter how badly you paint, so long as you don't paint badly like other people.

GEORGE MOORE

There is only one difference between a madman and me. I am not mad.

SALVADOR DALI

ATHLETES

Is it normal to wake up in the morning in a sweat because you can't wait to beat another human's guts out?

JOE KAPP

I'm throwing twice as hard as I ever did. The ball's just not going as fast.

LEFTY GOMEZ

What distinguishes certain players from others is the mental aspect.

MICHAEL JORDAN

An athlete has such a narrow view of life he does not know reality.

BRUCE JENNER

Look, when that crowd gets to cheering, when we know they're with us, when we know they like us, we play better. A hell of a lot better!

BILL CARLIN

It's hard not to play golf that's up to Jack Nicklaus standards when you *are* Jack Nicklaus.

JACK NICKLAUS

Too many people think an athlete's life can be an open book. You're supposed to be an example. Why do I have to be an example for your kid? You be an example for your kid.

BOB GIBSON

The problem with many athletes is they take themselves seriously and their sport lightly.

MIKE NEWLIN

Learn to compartmentalize yourself. You're an athlete for only a few more years. You have to live 80 or 90 years, so you better find more things to do.

TOM SANDERS

I wasn't always a terrific athlete. I can remember times when I couldn't run, jump and chew gum at the same time. And I just had to practice, practice, practice. I became a pretty good athlete after hard work.

SHAQUILLE O'NEAL

Didn't come up here to read. Came up here to hit.

HANK AARON

Attitude

If the only tool you have is a hammer, you tend to see every problem as a nail.

ALFRED ADLER

The only deadly sin I know is cynicism.

HENRY L. STIMSON

You can't sweep other people off their feet, if you can't be swept off your own.

CLARENCE DAY

Even smiling at someone, I feel as if I'm doing something to make the world a better place. I'd be doing that even if I weren't an actor.

DANNY GLOVER

All charming people usually have something to conceal, usually their total dependence on the appreciation of others.

CYRIL CONNOLLY

Constant kindness can accomplish much. As the sun makes ice melt, kindness causes misunderstanding, mistrust, and hostility to evaporate.

ALBERT SCHWEITZER

If you aren't fired with enthusiasm, you'll be fired with enthusiasm.

VINCE LOMBARDI

I'm not confused, I'm just well-mixed.

ROBERT FROST

If you feed on bitterness you can nitpick all the way to your death.

JAMES EARL JONES

Sadness is almost never anything but a form of fatigue.

ANDRÉ GIDE

I studied the lives of great men and women, and I found that the men and women who got to the top were those who did the jobs they had in hand, with everything they had of energy and enthusiasm and hard work.

HARRY S. TRUMAN

I don't know, I don't care, and it doesn't make any difference.

JACK KEROUAC

Belief

Some people will believe anything if you whisper it to them.

LOUIS B. NIZER

There are no atheists in the foxholes.

WILLIAM THOMAS CUMMINGS

We believe what we want to believe, what we like to believe, what suits our prejudices and fuels our passions.

SYDNEY J. HARRIS

One of the best paths to believability is understatement.

DANIEL J. BOORSTIN

There seems to be a terrible misunderstanding on the part of a great many people to the effect that when you cease to believe you may cease to behave.

LOUIS KRONENBERGER

I say that religion is the belief in future life and God. I don't believe in either.

CLARENCE S. DARROW

Any stigma is good enough to beat a dogma with.

PHILIP GUEDALLA

The belief in God is as necessary as sex.

ISAAC BASHEVIS SINGER

The Body

There is a wisdom in the body that is older and more reliable than clocks and calendars.

JOHN H. JOHNSON

My feet are dogs.

RUDOLF NUREYEV

I know from experience that the marriage of mind and body makes the sum more powerful than the individual parts.

GEORGE FOREMAN

I know a lot of athletes and models are written off as just bodies. I never felt used for my body.

ARNOLD SCHWARZENEGGER

Man consists of two parts, his mind and his body, only the body has more fun.

WOODY ALLEN

The hand is the cutting edge of the mind.

JACOB BRONOWSKI

I was taught that the human brain was the crowning glory of evolution so far, but I think it's a very poor scheme for survival.

KURT VONNEGUT

Anatomy is destiny.

SIGMUND FREUD

My brain is my second favorite organ.

WOODY ALLEN

Skin is like wax paper that holds everything in without dripping.

ART LINKLETTER

Books

A book must be an ice ax to break the frozen sea within us.

FRANZ KAFKA

Best-sellerism is the star system of the book world. A "best-seller" is a celebrity among books. It is a book known primarily (sometimes exclusively) for its well-knownness.

DANIEL J. BOORSTIN

A real book is not one that's read, but one that reads us.

W. H. AUDEN

Only two classes of books are of universal appeal. The very best and the very worst.

FORD MADOX FORD

It pains me to talk to a youngster who has never finished a book.

TOM BRADLEY

With a novelist, like a surgeon, you have to get a feeling that you've fallen into good hands—someone from whom you can accept the anesthetic with confidence.

SAUL BELLOW

From the moment I picked it [a book] up until I laid it down, I was convulsed with laughter. Some day I intend reading it.

GROUCHO MARX

The proper study of mankind is books.

ALDOUS HUXLEY

The possession of a book becomes a substitute for reading it.

ANTHONY BURGESS

Finishing a book is just like you took a child out in the back yard and shot it.

TRUMAN CAPOTE

Nothing is new except arrangement.

WILL DURANT

A truly great book should be read in youth, again in maturity and once more in old age, as a fine building should be seen by morning light, at noon and by moonlight.

ROBERTSON DAVIES

One tends to overpraise a long book because one has got through it.

E. M. FORSTER

The two biggest sellers in any bookstore are the cookbooks and the diet books. The cookbooks tell you how to prepare the food, and the diet books tell you how not to eat any of it.

ANDY ROONEY

Every novel should have a beginning, a muddle, and an end.

PETER DE VRIES

There is more treasure in books than in all the pirates' loot on Treasure Island . . . and best of all, you can enjoy these riches every day of your life.

WALT DISNEY

Some books are undeservedly forgotten; none are undeservedly remembered.

W. H. AUDEN

Bureaucracy

If you don't know what to do with many of the papers piled on your desk, stick a dozen colleagues' initials on 'em, and pass them along. When in doubt, route.

MALCOLM FORBES

There is something about a bureaucrat that does not like a poem.

GORE VIDAL

The longer the title, the less important the job.

GEORGE MCGOVERN

Dear Mrs., Mr., Miss or Mr. and Mrs. Daneeka: Words cannot express the deep personal grief I experienced when your husband, son, father or brother was killed, wounded or reported missing in action.

JOSEPH HELLER

The only thing that saves us from bureaucracy is its inefficiency.

EUGENE MCCARTHY

The hardest thing in the world to understand is the income tax.

ALBERT EINSTEIN

Committee—a group of men who keep minutes and waste hours.

MILTON BERLE

Even Albert Einstein reportedly needed help on his 1040 form.

RONALD REAGAN

Whenever you have an efficient government you have a dictatorship.

HARRY S. TRUMAN

The volume of paper expands to fill the available briefcase.

JERRY BROWN

Business

He's a businessman . . . I'll make him an offer he can't refuse.

MARIO PUZO

A business that makes nothing but money is a poor kind of business.

HENRY FORD

Whenever you're sitting across from some important person, always picture him sitting there in a suit of long red underwear. That's the way I always operated in business.

JOSEPH P. KENNEDY

Is baseball a business? If it isn't, General Motors is a sport.

JIM MURRAY

The three-martini lunch is the epitome of American efficiency. Where else can you get an earful, a bellyful and a snootful at the same time?

GERALD R. FORD

A verbal agreement isn't worth the paper it's written on.

SAMUEL GOLDWYN

The secret in business is to know something that nobody else knows.

ARISTOTLE ONASSIS

Dream, diversify—and never miss an angle.

WALT DISNEY

My rackets are run on strictly American lines and they're going to stay that way.

AL CAPONE

Deals are my art form. Other people paint beautifully on canvas or write wonderful poetry. I like making deals, preferably big deals. That's how I get my kicks.

DONALD TRUMP

Capital Punishment

The compensation for a death sentence is knowledge of the exact hour when one is to die. A great luxury, but one that is well earned.

VLADIMIR NABOKOV

When I came back to Dublin, I was courtmartialled in my absence and sentenced to death in my absence, so I said they could shoot me in my absence.

BRENDAN BEHAN

Human rights mean that unsuitable individuals should be liquidated so that others can live free.

SADEQ KHALKHALI

Let us call it by the name which, for lack of any other nobility, will at least give the nobility of truth, and let us recognize it for what it essentially is: revenge.

ALBERT CAMUS

These death sentences are cruel and unusual in the same way that being struck by lightning is cruel and unusual.

POTTER STEWART

Capital punishment is either an affront to humanity or a potential parking place.

LARRY BROWN

The California executioner keeps banker's hours. He never kills before 10 o'clock in the morning, never after 4 in the afternoon.

CARYL CHESSMAN

So long as governments set the example of killing their enemies, private individuals will occasionally kill theirs.

ELBERT HUBBARD

CAREERS

There are more pleasant things to do than beat up people.

MUHAMMAD ALI

The secret of long life is double careers. One to about age sixty, then another for the next thirty years.

DAVID OGILVY

It almost looks as if analysis were the third of those "impossible" professions in which one can be quite sure of unsatisfying results. The other two, much older-established, are the bringing-up of children and the government of nations.

SIGMUND FREUD

If you get to thirty-five and your job still involves wearing a name tag, you've probably made a serious vocational error.

DENNIS MILLER

Give me a dozen healthy infants, well-formed, and my own specialized world to bring them up in and I'll guarantee to take any one at random and train him to become any type of specialist I might select—doctor, lawyer, artist, merchant chief and, yes, even beggarman and thief, regardless of his talents, penchants, tendencies, abilities, vocations, and race of his ancestors.

JOHN B. WATSON

People don't choose their careers; they are engulfed by them.

JOHN DOS PASSOS

I would have made a good Pope.

RICHARD M. NIXON

Today, being a cowboy is more an attitude than an occupation.

BOBBY BARE

The test of a vocation is the love of the drudgery it involves.

LOGAN PEARSALL SMITH

Hurting people is my business.

SUGAR RAY ROBINSON

The difference between a job and a career is the difference between forty and sixty hours a week.

ROBERT FROST

I should have been a country-western singer. After all, I'm older than most western countries.

GEORGE BURNS

Old soldiers never die; they just fade away.

DOUGLAS MACARTHUR

The doctor can bury his mistakes but an architect can only advise his client to plant vines.

FRANK LLOYD WRIGHT

A musician must make music, an artist must paint, a poet must write, if he is to be ultimately at peace with himself. What a man can be, he must be.

ABRAHAM MASLOW

Censorship

I call upon the intellectual community in this country and abroad to stand up for freedom of imagination, an issue much larger than my book or indeed my life.

SALMAN RUSHDIE

If we value the pursuit of knowledge, we must be free to follow wherever that search may lead us. The free mind is no barking dog to be tethered on a ten-foot chain.

ADLAI E. STEVENSON

Not everything's for children. Not everything's for everyone.

ROBERT CRUMB

As long as federal dollars are used to finance art projects, Congress will have the responsibility to its constituents to determine what type of art taxpayer dollars will support.

PHILIP M. CRANE

When there is official censorship it is a sign that speech is serious. When there is none, it is pretty certain that the official spokesmen have all the loudspeakers.

PAUL GOODMAN

Did you ever hear anyone say "that work had better be banned, because I might read it and it might be very damaging to me"?

JOSEPH HENRY JACKSON

They can't censor the gleam in my eye.

CHARLES LAUGHTON

Vietnam was the first war ever fought without any censorship. Without censorship, things can get terribly confused in the public mind.

WILLIAM WESTMORELAND

Censorship reflects a society's lack of confidence in itself.

POTTER STEWART

CHALLENGES

The challenge is to turn midnight into days, pain into power. If you're swimming, and there's a stiff wind and a vicious storm coming, you can't stop swimming and explain the storm away. You've got to keep kicking.

JESSE JACKSON

Problems are just opportunities in work clothes.

HENRY KAISER

There is nothing I like better than a challenge.

MUGGSY BOGUES

A problem is a chance for you to do your best.

DUKE ELLINGTON

I have yet to see any problem, however complicated, which, when you looked at it in the right way, did not become still more complicated.

POUL ANDERSON

We fight for lost causes because we know that our defeat and dismay may be the preface to our successors' victory, though that victory itself will be temporary; we fight rather to keep something alive than in the expectation that anything will triumph.

T. S. ELIOT

When you get to the end of your rope, tie a knot so's you can hang on.

JAMES MITCHELL

I believe the greater the handicap the greater the triumph.

JOHN H. JOHNSON

If there is a possibility of several things going wrong, the one that will cause the most damage will be the one to go wrong.

ARTHUR BLOCH

In crisis the most daring course is often the safest.

HENRY KISSINGER

The best way out is always through.

ROBERT FROST

CHANGE

It is the nature of man as he grows older to protest against change, particularly change for the better.

JOHN STEINBECK

Elders always lament change—and the young cannot wait for it.

MALCOLM FORBES

Every moment of one's existence one is growing into more or retreating into less. One is always living a little more or dying a little less.

NORMAN MAILER

Things don't change. You change your way of looking, that's all.

CARLOS CASTANEDA

Change is the law of life. And those who look only to the past or the present are certain to miss the future.

JOHN F. KENNEDY

There is a time for departure even when there's no certain place to go.

TENNESSEE WILLIAMS

Progress is a nice word. But change is its motivator and change is its enemy.

ROBERT F. KENNEDY

There is nothing wrong with change, if it is in the right direction.

WINSTON CHURCHILL

Happiness is never really so welcome as changelessness.

GRAHAM GREENE

Most of us are about as eager to be changed as we were to be born, and go through our changes in a similar state of shock.

JAMES BALDWIN

The basic fact of today is the tremendous pace of change in human life.

JAWAHARLAL NEHRU

The only completely consistent people are dead.

ALDOUS HUXLEY

Wisdom lies neither in fixity nor in change, but in the dialectic between the two.

OCTAVIO PAZ

CHILDHOOD

Childhood is a disease—a sickness that you grow out of.

WILLIAM GOLDING

I cannot think of any need in childhood as strong as the need for a father's protection.

SIGMUND FREUD

I was raised by just my mom. See, my father died when I was eight years old. At least, that's what he told us in the letter.

DREW CAREY

I am convinced that, except in a few extraordinary cases, one form or another of an unhappy childhood is essential to the formation of exceptional gifts.

THORNTON WILDER

When I was a child what I wanted to be when I grew up was an invalid.

QUENTIN CRISP

I was caesarean born. You can't really tell, although whenever I leave a house, I go through the window.

STEVEN WRIGHT

We were so poor, every Christmas Eve my old man would go outside and shoot his gun, then come in and tell us kids that Santa Claus had committed suicide.

JAKE LAMOTTA

When you are eight years old, nothing is any of your business.

LENNY BRUCE

CHILDREN

To love children is to love God.

ROY ROGERS

Your children need your presence more than your presents.

JESSE JACKSON

What is youth except a man or woman before it is fit to be seen?

EVELYN WAUGH

When we look at actual children, no matter how they are raised, we notice immediately that little girls are in fact smaller versions of real human beings, whereas little boys are Pod People from the Planet Destructo.

DAVE BARRY

If a child shows himself incorrigible, he should be decently and quietly beheaded at the age of twelve.

DON MARQUIS

A baby is God's opinion that the world should go on.

CARL SANDBURG

Raising children is part joy and part guerilla warfare.

ED ASNER

Yes, having a child is surely the most beautifully irrational act that two people in love can commit.

BILL COSBY

Ah, the patter of little feet around the house. There's nothing like having a midget for a butler.

W. C. FIELDS

Training a child is more or less a matter of pot luck.

ROD MACLEAN

One of the most obvious facts about grown-ups to a child is that they have forgotten what it is like to be a child.

RANDALL JARRELL

Blessed are the young, for they shall inherit the national debt.

HERBERT HOOVER

[I play hard] because there is always some kid who may be seeing me for the first or last time. I owe him my best.

JOE DIMAGGIO

Youth is such a wonderful thing. What a crime to waste it on children.

GEORGE BERNARD SHAW

It is no wonder that people are so horrible when they start life as children.

KINGSLEY AMIS

There are children playing in the street who could solve some of my top problems in physics, because they have modes of sensory perception that I lost long ago.

J. ROBERT OPPENHEIMER

Your children are not your children.
They are the sons and daughters of Life's longing for itself.

KAHLIL GIBRAN

Children have never been very good at listening to their elders, but they have never failed to imitate them.

JAMES BALDWIN

Insanity is hereditary; you can get it from your children.

SAM LEVENSON

A child is nature's only bona fide, guaranteed positive surprise.

JACK NICHOLSON

I know fame and power are for the birds. But then suddenly life comes into focus for me. And, ah, there stand my kids. I love them.

LEE IACOCCA

COMPETITION

You never get ahead of anyone as long as you try to get even with him.

LOU HOLTZ

Men often compete with one another until the day they die; comradeship consists of rubbing shoulders jocularly with a competitor.

EDWARD HOAGLAND

I don't meet competition. I crush it.

CHARLES REVSON

Don't knock your competitors. By boosting others you will boost yourself. A little competition is a good thing and severe competition is a blessing. Thank God for competition.

JACOB KINDLEBERGER

To knock a thing down, especially if it is cocked at an arrogant angle, is a deep delight to the blood.

GEORGE SANTAYANA

When you are not practicing, remember, someone somewhere is practicing, and when you meet him he will win.

ED MACAULEY

The world is divided into people who do things and people who get the credit. Try, if you can, to belong to the first class. There's far less competition.

DWIGHT MORROW

The trouble in American life today, in business as well as sports, is that too many people are afraid of competition. The result is that, in some circles, people have come to sneer at success, if it costs hard work and training and sacrifice.

KNUTE ROCKNE

Without the spur of competition we'd loaf out our life.

ARNOLD GLASOW

CONSERVATIVES

They define themselves in terms of what they oppose.

GEORGE F. WILL

A conservative is a man with two perfectly good legs who, however, has never learned to walk forward.

FRANKLIN D. ROOSEVELT

The intelligent conservative combines a disposition to preserve with an ability to reform.

RUSSELL KIRK

A liberal is a person who believes that water can be made to run uphill. A conservative is someone who believes everybody should pay for his water. I'm somewhere in between: I believe water should be free, but that it flows downhill.

THEODORE H. WHITE

We're not winning because we hide who we are. We're winning because we advertise who we are. We don't have to pretend to be mainstream. We are mainstream.

RALPH REED

A conservative is someone who demands a square deal for the rich.

DAVID FROST

I never dared be a radical when young
For fear it would make me conservative when old.

ROBERT FROST

Consumerism

Living is more a question of what one spends than what one makes.

MARCEL DUCHAMP

Increase of material comforts, it may be generally laid down, does not in any way whatsoever conduce to moral growth.

MAHATMA GANDHI

Playboy linked sex with upward mobility. If you can make people feel it's OK to enjoy themselves, you've got a winning product—whatever it is.

HUGH HEFNER

What's great about this country is that America started the tradition where the richest consumers buy essentially the same things as the poorest.

ANDY WARHOL

You really have to wonder why we even bother to get *up* in the morning. I mean, really: *Why work?* Simply to buy more *stuff*?

DOUGLAS COUPLAND

In our rich consumers' civilization we spin cocoons around ourselves and get possessed by our possessions.

MAX LERNER

In the factory we make cosmetics. In the store we sell hope.

CHARLES REVSON

CONVERSATION AND COMMUNICATION

Talk low, talk slow, and don't say too much.

JOHN WAYNE

Too much agreement kills a chat.

ELDRIDGE CLEAVER

It's better to be quiet and ignorant than to open your mouth and remove all doubt.

JOHN MCNAMARA

Conversation would be vastly improved by the constant use of four simple words: I do not know.

ANDRÉ MAUROIS

The right to be heard does not automatically include the right to be taken seriously.

HUBERT HUMPHREY

Hanging is too good for a man who makes puns; he should be drawn and quoted.

FRED ALLEN

Jaw-jaw is better than war-war.

HAROLD MACMILLAN

Practically anything you say will seem amusing if you're on all fours.

P. J. O'ROURKE

Speech is civilization itself. The word . . . preserves contact—
it is silence which isolates.

THOMAS MANN

Let us never negotiate out of fear; but let us never fear to
negotiate.

JOHN F. KENNEDY

Every man becomes, to a certain degree, what the people
he generally converses with are.

PHILIP DORMER STANHOPE

Next to being witty yourself, the best thing is to quote another's wit.

CHRISTIAN N. BOVEE

No one gossips about other people's secret virtues.

BERTRAND RUSSELL

Nothing I have said is factual except the bits that sound
like fiction.

CLIVE JAMES

A conversation is a dialogue, not a monologue. That's why
there are so few good conversations: due to scarcity, two
intelligent talkers seldom meet.

TRUMAN CAPOTE

Whenever you accept our views we shall be in full agreement with you.

MOSHE DAYAN

The trouble with telling a good story is that it invariably reminds the other fellow of a bad one.

SID CAESAR

I often quote myself. It adds spice to my conversations.

GEORGE BERNARD SHAW

COURAGE

Courage is contagious. When a brave man takes a stand, the spines of others are often stiffened.

BILLY GRAHAM

Life has made me brave.

BILL T. JONES

Courage is doing what you're afraid to do. There can be no courage unless you are scared.

GEORGE S. PATTON

The first and great commandment is, Don't let them scare you.

ELMER DAVIS

Courage in days gone by meant taking your own part, fighting your own battles. On the range, you handled yourself. It was part of the code.

C. L. SONNICHSEN

What counts is not necessarily the size of the dog in the fight—it's the size of the fight in the dog.

DWIGHT D. EISENHOWER

The important thing when you are going to do something brave is to have someone on hand who will witness it.

MICHAEL HOWARD

What would life be like if we had no courage to attempt anything?

VINCENT VAN GOGH

CREATIVITY

When you're creating your own shit . . . even the sky ain't the limit.

MILES DAVIS

Our inventions mirror our secret wishes.

LAWRENCE DURRELL

Creativity, not destruction, should be the yardstick of greatness.

FELA ANIKULAPO KUTI

The unconscious mind has a habit of asserting itself in the afternoon.

ANTHONY BURGESS

Man unites himself with the world in the process of creation.

ERICH FROMM

All men are creative but few are artists.

PAUL GOODMAN

A hunch is creativity trying to tell you something.

FRANK CAPRA

Make what you'd like to hear first. What turns you on. Because you can't figure out what people are going to like.

QUINCY JONES

All you have to do is close your eyes and wait for the symbols.

TENNESSEE WILLIAMS

All I need to make a comedy is a park, a policeman and a pretty girl.

CHARLIE CHAPLIN

Don't think! Thinking is the enemy of creativity. It's self-conscious, and anything self-conscious is lousy. You can't try to do things; you simply must do them.

RAY BRADBURY

It's not the public that inspires an artist to create. An artist feels the need to create even if there is no public. If there were no one on the planet I'd still do funny things. I'd just be laughing by myself.

EDDIE MURPHY

CRIME

I think crime pays. The hours are good, you travel a lot.

WOODY ALLEN

It's better to be wanted for murder than not to be wanted at all.

MARTY WINCH

New York now leads the world's great cities in the number of people around whom you shouldn't make a sudden move.

DAVID LETTERMAN

I hate this "crime doesn't pay" stuff. Crime in the United States is perhaps one of the biggest businesses in the world today.

PETER KIRK

Don't you get the idea that I'm one of those goddamn radicals. Don't get the idea that I'm knocking the American system.

AL CAPONE

I was going to read the report about the rising crime rate . . . but somebody stole it.

WILL ROGERS

The criminal is not alone when he returns to the scene of the crime; he is joined there by his victim, and both are driven by the same curiosity: to relive that moment which stamped past and future for each.

ELIE WIESEL

People have got to know whether or not their president is a crook. Well, I'm not a crook. I earned everything I've got.

RICHARD M. NIXON

Thieves respect property. They merely wish the property to become their property that they may more perfectly respect it.

G. K. CHESTERTON

CRITICS AND CRITICISM

To avoid criticism, say nothing, do nothing, be nothing.
FRED SHERO

Time is the only critic without ambition.
JOHN STEINBECK

Criticism is prejudice made plausible.
H. L. MENCKEN

A critic is a gong at a railroad crossing clanging loudly and vainly as the train goes by.
CHRISTOPHER MORLEY

Capitalize upon criticism. It's one of the hardest things in the world to accept criticism, especially when it's not presented in a constructive way, and turn it to your advantage.
J. C. PENNEY

Book reviewers are little old ladies of both sexes.
JOHN O'HARA

I'd much rather be liked by the people than by critics. Much better.

BERNARD BUFFET

I can take any amount of criticism, so long as it is unqualified praise.

NOEL COWARD

Any reviewer who expresses rage and loathing for a novel is preposterous. He or she is like a person who has put on full armor and attacked a hot fudge sundae.

KURT VONNEGUT

You can read 25 positive things about yourself and feel great and then hear one negative thing that's a lie, and it bothers the hell out of you.

BERRY GORDY, JR.

When you soar like an eagle, you attract the hunters.

MILTON S. GOULD

Critics are like eunuchs in a harem. They're there every night, they see it done every night, they see how it should be done every night, but they can't do it themselves.

BRENDAN BEHAN

Honest criticism is hard to take, particularly from a relative, a friend, an acquaintance or a stranger.

FRANKLIN P. JONES

Dance

Dance is the only art of which we ourselves are the stuff of which it is made.

TED SHAWN

May I have the pleasure of the next sadly outdated courting ritual.

MICHAEL LEUNING

I'm going to tap dance until I can't.

GREGORY HINES

To shake your rump is to be environmentally aware.

DAVID BYRNE

Physically, dancing hurts. There are always varying degrees of comfort and pain.

ALVIN AILEY

I just put my feet in the air and move them around.

FRED ASTAIRE

Teenagers and old people may know how to dance, but real people who go to real parties haven't the slightest. The only dances they even half remember how to do are the ones they learned twenty years ago. This is what the old Supremes tape is for: stiff and overweight versions of the Jerk, the Mashed Potato, the Pony, the Swim, and the Watusi. And after six drinks everyone will revert to the Twist.

P. J. O'ROURKE

Dancing is a perpendicular expression of a horizontal desire.

GEORGE BERNARD SHAW

Death

A single death is a tragedy, a million deaths is a statistic.

JOSEPH STALIN

I am ready to meet my Maker. Whether my Maker is prepared for the ordeal of meeting me is another matter.

WINSTON CHURCHILL

Death is just a distant rumor to the young.

ANDY ROONEY

There's no reason to be the richest man in the cemetery. You can't do any business from there.

COLONEL SANDERS

For three days after death hair and fingernails continue to grow but phone calls taper off.

JOHNNY CARSON

I think about dying. I've come to realize we all die alone in one way or another. You can have a room full of people when it's your time to walk into the light, but you can bet your ass not one person will offer to go with you.

RICHARD PRYOR

Death . . . It's the only thing we haven't succeeded in completely vulgarizing.

ALDOUS HUXLEY

Do not go gentle into that good night,
Old age should burn and rave at close of day;
Rage, rage against the dying of the light.

DYLAN THOMAS

They say such nice things about people at their funerals that it makes me sad to realize that I'm going to miss mine by just a few days.

GARRISON KEILLOR

The graveyards are full of indispensable men.

CHARLES DE GAULLE

I wouldn't mind dying in a plane crash. It would be a good way to go. I don't want to die of old age or OD or drift off in my sleep. I want to feel what it's like. I want to taste it, hear it, smell it. Death is only going to happen once, right. I don't want to miss it.

JIM MORRISON

If my doctor told me I only had six minutes to live, I wouldn't brood. I'd type a little faster.

ISAAC ASIMOV

No one believes in his own death, or, to put the same thing in another way, that in the unconscious every man of us is convinced of his own immortality.

SIGMUND FREUD

We know we all want to go to heaven but nobody wants to die.

MR. T

I'm not afraid to die. I just don't want to be there when it happens.

WOODY ALLEN

Death comes along like a gas bill one can't pay—and that's all one can say about it.

ANTHONY BURGESS

Democracy

The sound of tireless voices is the price we pay for the right to hear the music of our own opinions.

ADLAI E. STEVENSON

Vote early and vote often.

AL CAPONE

Democracy means government by discussion but it is only effective if you can stop people talking.

CLEMENT ATTLEE

Democracy is not a fragile flower: still, it needs cultivating.

RONALD REAGAN

Democracy is the theory that the common people know what they want, and deserve to get it good and hard.

H. L. MENCKEN

It has been said that democracy is the worst form of government except all the others that have been tried.

WINSTON CHURCHILL

Elections are won by men and women chiefly because most people vote against somebody rather than for somebody.

FRANKLIN P. ADAMS

A democracy is the most difficult kind of government to operate. It represents the last flowering, really, of the human experience.

JOHN F. KENNEDY

Two cheers for democracy: one because it admits variety and two because it permits criticism.

E. M. FORSTER

Democracy demands that all of its citizens begin the race even. Egalitarianism insists that they all *finish* even.

ROGER PRICE

Democracy is not a static thing. It is an everlasting march.

FRANKLIN D. ROOSEVELT

The more you encourage someone else's freedom of expression and the more different that someone else is from you, the more democratic the act.

WYNTON MARSALIS

Constantly choosing the lesser of two evils is still choosing evil.

JERRY GARCIA

Divorce

We pondered whether to take a vacation or get a divorce and decided that a trip to Bermuda is over in two weeks, but a divorce is something you always have.

WOODY ALLEN

The happiest time of anyone's life is just after the first divorce.

JOHN KENNETH GALBRAITH

Honesty has ruined more marriages than infidelity.

CHARLES MCCABE

You never realize how short a month is until you pay alimony.

JOHN BARRYMORE

Divorce is a game played by lawyers.

CARY GRANT

No one is going to take women's liberation seriously until women recognize that they will not be thought of as equals in the secret privacy of men's most private mental parts until they eschew alimony.

NORMAN MAILER

She cried—and the judge wiped her tears with my check-book.

TOMMY MANVILLE

Divorce. Termination of a marriage before either spouse can terminate the other. According to custom, both parties enter into a knockdown legal battle that is always won by their attorneys and usually lost by their children.

RICK BAYAN

Doctors

Show me a sane man and I will cure him for you.

CARL JUNG

A psychiatrist is the next man you start talking to after you start talking to yourself.

FRED ALLEN

Keep away from physicians. It is all probing and guessing and pretending with them. They leave it to Nature to cure in her own time, but they take the credit. As well as very fat fees.

ANTHONY BURGESS

The best doctor in the world is the Veterinarian. He can't ask his patients what is the matter—he's just got to know.

WILL ROGERS

My doctor gave me six months to live but when I couldn't pay the bill, he gave me six months more.

WALTER MATTHAU

The fact that doctors themselves die of the very diseases they profess to cure passes unnoticed.

GEORGE BERNARD SHAW

Doctors and lawyers must go to school for years and years, often with little sleep and with great sacrifice to their first wives.

ROY BLOUNT, JR.

My psychiatrist and I have decided that when we both think I'm ready, I'm going to get in my car and drive off the Verranzo Bridge.

NEIL SIMON

My doctor is wonderful. Once, in 1955, when I couldn't afford an operation, he touched up the X-rays.

JOEY BISHOP

Remember, half the doctors in the country graduated in the bottom half of the class.

AL MCGUIRE

Dreams

We do not really feel grateful towards those who make our dreams come true; they ruin our dreams.

ERIC HOFFER

Hold fast to dreams, for if dreams die, life is a broken-winged bird that cannot fly.

LANGSTON HUGHES

Man is not the sum of what he has but the totality of what he does not yet have, of what he might have.

JEAN-PAUL SARTRE

I went a lot of days without food to eat; I went a lot of days and even weeks wearing the same clothing and the only thing that kept me going was my dream.

MR. T

Living at risk is jumping off the cliff and building your own wings on the way down.

RAY BRADBURY

But a man who doesn't dream is like a man who doesn't sweat. He stores up a lot of poison.

TRUMAN CAPOTE

When you cease to dream you cease to live.

MALCOLM FORBES

Make strong old dreams lest this our world lose heart.

EZRA POUND

Dreamers are insatiable expansionists, and the space of dreams rapidly becomes overcrowded.

JOHN ASHBERY

It has been my experience—and this I have found no exception—that every dream treats of oneself. Dreams are absolutely egoistic.

SIGMUND FREUD

People who insist on telling their dreams are among the terrors of the breakfast table.

MAX BEERBOHM

Dreaming permits each and every one of us to be quietly and safely insane every night of our lives.

WILLIAM DEMENT

Drugs

Cocaine is God's way of saying you're making too much money.

ROBIN WILLIAMS

I give so much pleasure to so many people. Why can I not get some pleasure for myself? Why do I have to stop?

JOHN BELUSHI

Drugs are wrong. They burn out your brain and they sear your soul.

WILLIAM J. BENNETT

The only reason that cocaine is such a rage today is that people are too dumb and lazy to get themselves together to roll a joint.

JACK NICHOLSON

You are either on the bus or off the bus.

KEN KESEY

A drug is neither moral nor immoral—it's a chemical compound. The compound itself is not a menace to society until a human being treats it as if consumption bestowed a temporary license to act like an asshole.

FRANK ZAPPA

If God had wanted us high, He would have given us wings.

ARSENIO HALL

Drugs have taught an entire generation of American kids the metric system.

P. J. O'ROURKE

Drugs are nihilistic; they undermine all values and radically overturn all our ideas about good and evil, what is just and what is unjust, what is permitted and what is forbidden.

OCTAVIO PAZ

Turn on, tune in, drop out.

TIMOTHY LEARY

Every form of addiction is bad, no matter whether the narcotic be alcohol or morphine or idealism.

CARL JUNG

I hate to advocate drugs, alcohol, violence, or insanity to anyone, but they've always worked for me.

HUNTER S. THOMPSON

And the answer on drugs is, again, education—until some genius finds an antidote that you can stick in your arm and it does away with all addictions.

MARIO CUOMO

I'll die young but it's like kissing God.

LENNY BRUCE

Avoid all needle drugs—the only dope worth shooting is Richard Nixon.

ABBIE HOFFMAN

Yes, I tried marijuana in England, but I didn't like it. And I didn't inhale.

WILLIAM J. CLINTON

Education

If you think education is expensive, try ignorance.

DEREK BOK

The mere imparting of information is not education. Above all things, the effort must result in making a man do and think for himself.

CARTER G. WOODSON

Anyone who stops learning is old, whether at twenty or eighty. Anyone who keeps learning stays young. The greatest thing in life is to keep your mind young.

HENRY FORD

Education is what survives when what has been learnt has been forgotten.

B. F. SKINNER

A liberal education . . . frees a man from the prison-house of his class, race, time, place, background, family, and even his nation.

ROBERT MAYNARD HUTCHINS

Once you're educated, no one can steal what's in your mind.

DON KING

Education is our passport to the future, for tomorrow belongs to the people who prepare for it today.

MALCOLM X

There are obviously two educations. One should teach us how to make a living and the other how to live.

JAMES TRUSLOW ADAMS

I tell my sons to never take anything for granted; that education is the key to release the shackles of slavery, be it years ago or today.

SUGAR RAY LEONARD

Education is a weapon whose effect depends on who holds it in his hands and at whom it is aimed.

JOSEPH STALIN

Nobody owes you anything. But you can go out and take it. With education. Pick up a book and read. Learn your history and everybody else's too. And don't be scared to be yourself.

SINBAD

School is always in session.

PHILIP ALLEN

Knowledge does not keep any better than fish.

ALFRED NORTH WHITEHEAD

If I ran a school, I'd give the average grade to the ones who gave men all the right answers, for being good parrots. I'd give the top grades to those who made a lot of mistakes and told me about them, and then told me what they learned from them.

R. BUCKMINSTER FULLER

To sow schools is to reap men.

FIDEL CASTRO

Education is hanging around until you've caught on.

ROBERT FROST

When I finished school I took one of those career aptitude tests and, based on my verbal ability score, they suggested I become a mime.

TIM CAVANAUGH

I graduated from the college of the street. I got a Ph.D. in how to make ends meet.

QUINCY JONES

Before I came here I was confused about this subject. Having listened to your lecture I am still confused. But on a higher level.

ENRICO FERMI

There are no such things as limits to growth, because there are no limits on the human capacity for intelligence, imagination and wonder.

RONALD REAGAN

Egotism

Be humble or you'll stumble.

DWIGHT MOODY

I'm in trouble because I'm normal and slightly arrogant. A lot of people don't like themselves and I happen to be totally in love with myself.

MIKE TYSON

There's no such thing as bragging. You're either lying or telling the truth.

AL OLIVER

I'm happenin'.

GEORGE FOREMAN

I'm the Connie Francis of rock and roll.

ELTON JOHN

I was probably the only revolutionary ever referred to as "cute."

ABBIE HOFFMAN

I'm the greatest.

MUHAMMAD ALI

The longer I live the more I see that I am never wrong about anything, and that all the pains I have so humbly taken to verify my notions have only wasted my time.

GEORGE BERNARD SHAW

When men think they are like gods they are usually much less than men, being conceited fools.

D. H. LAWRENCE

If I only had a little humility, I would be perfect.

TED TURNER

I was very embarrassed when my canvases began to fetch high prices. I saw myself condemned to a future of nothing but masterpieces.

HENRI MATISSE

The only demand I make of my reader is that he should devote his whole life to reading my works.

JAMES JOYCE

I am a deeply superficial person.

ANDY WARHOL

I'm not crazy, but I think everyone else is.

PETER O'TOOLE

I happened to catch my reflection the other day when I was polishing my trophies, and, gee, it's easy to see why women are nuts about me.

TOM RYAN

If you have no confidence in self you are twice defeated in the race of life. With confidence you have won even before you have started.

MARCUS GARVEY

Environment

Plant trees. They give us two of the most crucial elements for our survival: oxygen and books.

A. WHITNEY BROWN

I hate the outdoors. To me the outdoors is where the car is.

WILL DURST

We've been treating Mother Earth the way some people treat a rental apartment. Just trash it and move on.

MICHAEL JACKSON

A river has no politics.

DAVID E. LILIENTHAL

People are only beginning to realize that we are part of nature, not outside it. We are beginning to understand that instead of conquering nature, we must live in harmony with it.

EDWARD M. KENNEDY

The planting of trees is the least self-centered of all we can do. It is a purer act of faith than the procreation of children.

THORNTON WILDER

Man is messy, but any creature that can create space vehicles can probably cope.

GEORGE F. WILL

It's a morbid observation, but if everyone on earth just stopped breathing for an hour, the greenhouse effect would no longer be a problem.

JERRY ADLER

I just come and talk to the plants, really—very important to talk to them, they respond I find.

CHARLES, PRINCE OF WALES

We are all passengers aboard one ship, the Earth, and we must not allow it to be wrecked. There will be no second Noah's ark.

MIKHAIL GORBACHEV

There's so much pollution in the air now that if it weren't for our lungs there'd be no place to put it all.

ROBERT ORBEN

Our loyalties are to the species and the planet. *We* speak for Earth. Our obligation to survive is owed not just to ourselves but also to that Cosmos, ancient and vast, from which we spring.

CARL SAGAN

Today I have grown taller from walking with the trees.

KARL BAKER

And from the ancient forests of Oregon, to the Inland Empire of California, America's great middle class has got to start standing up to the environmental extremists who put insects, rats and birds ahead of families, workers, and jobs.

PATRICK BUCHANAN

The people most affected by environmental policy aren't born yet.

ROBERT F. KENNEDY

In its deepest sense, the environmentalism that concerns itself with the ecology of the whole earth is rising powerfully from the part of our being that knows better, that knows to consolidate, protect, and conserve those things which we care about before we manipulate and change them, perhaps irrevocably.

AL GORE

I would hate to pass through a planet and not leave it a better place.

SUN RA

Equality and Freedom

Until justice is blind to color, until education is unaware of race, until opportunity ceases to squint its eyes at pigmentation of human complexions, emancipation will be a proclamation—but it will not be a fact.

LYNDON B. JOHNSON

Freedom's just another word for nothing left to lose.

KRIS KRISTOFFERSON

To be truly free is to clearly see the depths of life. This demands that you step to the edge of a slippery cliff. Few avoid falling over, and the bottom down below has no cushion.

CORNEL WEST

Equality
I spoke the word
As if a wedding vow
Ah, but I was so much older then
I'm younger than that now.

BOB DYLAN

It's often safer to be in chains than to be free.

FRANZ KAFKA

Freedom is not something that anybody can be given, freedom is something that people take.

JAMES BALDWIN

You can only protect your liberties in this world by protecting other men's freedom. You can only be free if I am free.

CLARENCE S. DARROW

As for me, I am against freedom. I am for the blessed Inquisition. Freedom is shit, and that's why all these countries founder, from an excess of liberty.

SALVADOR DALI

You cannot separate peace from freedom, because no one can be at peace unless he has his freedom.

MALCOLM X

I know but one freedom and that is freedom of the mind.

ANTOINE DE SAINT-EXUPÉRY

I have a dream that one day this nation will rise up, live out the true meaning of its creed: we hold these truths to be self-evident, that all men are created equal.

MARTIN LUTHER KING, JR.

We must be thoroughly democratic and patronise everybody without distinction of class.

GEORGE BERNARD SHAW

Quotas don't help anyone. In fact, they are one of the worst forms of racial and gender-based discrimination. Every American citizen should be treated equally and should have equal opportunity under the law.

ALFONSE D'AMATO

The real value of freedom is not to the minority, that wants to talk, but to the majority, that does not want to listen.

ZECHARIAH CHAFEE, JR.

Ethics

We must learn to distinguish morality from moralizing.

HENRY KISSINGER

Living with a conscience is like driving a car with the brakes on.

BUDD SCHULBERG

If it ever came to a choice between compromising my moral principles and the performance of my duties, I know I'd go with my moral principles.

NORMAN SCHWARZKOPF

We do many things at the federal level that would be considered dishonest and illegal if done in the private sector.

DONALD REGAN

The force that rules the world is conduct, whether it be moral or immoral.

NICHOLAS MURRAY BUTLER

He who wears his morality but as his best garment were better naked.

KAHLIL GIBRAN

There can be no question of holding forth on ethics. I have seen people behave badly with great morality and I note every day that integrity has no need of rules.

ALBERT CAMUS

A man's ethical behavior should be based effectually on sympathy, education, and social ties; no religious basis is necessary. Man would indeed be in a poor way if he had to be restrained by fear of punishment and hope of reward after death.

ALBERT EINSTEIN

Everyone has his own conscience, and there should be no rules about how a conscience should function.

ERNEST HEMINGWAY

Moral indignation is jealousy with a halo.

H. G. WELLS

There's right and there's wrong. You get to do one or the other. You do the one, and you're living. You do the other, and you may be walking around, but you're dead as a beaver hat.

JOHN WAYNE

I would rather be the man who bought the Brooklyn Bridge than the man who sold it.

WILL ROGERS

The difference between a moral man and a man of honor is that the latter regrets a discreditable act, even when it has worked and he has not been caught.

H. L. MENCKEN

Morality is largely a matter of geography.

ELBERT HUBBARD

EXERCISE

Push-ups, sit-ups, run in place.
Each night I keep a grueling pace.
With bleak results, I must divulge—
I've lost the battle of the bulge.

CHARLES GHINGA

Exercise is bunk. If you are healthy you don't need it; if you are sick you shouldn't take it.

HENRY FORD

[On how to live a long life] "Take a two-mile walk every morning before breakfast."

HARRY S. TRUMAN

We can now prove that large numbers of Americans are dying from sitting on their behinds.

BRUCE B. DAN

Use it or lose it.

JIMMY CONNORS

I like long walks, especially when they are taken by people who annoy me.

FRED ALLEN

Whenever I feel like exercise, I lie down until the feeling passes.

ROBERT MAYNARD HUTCHINS

Can't eat without exercise.

GEORGE FOREMAN

People seem to think there is something inherently noble and virtuous in the desire to go for a walk.

MAX BEERBOHM

Experience

Judgment comes from experience and great judgment comes from bad experience.

ROBERT PACKWOOD

Life is a succession of lessons enforced by immediate reward, or, oftener, by immediate chastisement.

ERNEST DIMNET

Everything happens to everybody sooner or later if there is time enough.

GEORGE BERNARD SHAW

Experience is something I always think I have until I get more of it.

BURTON HILLIS

We are a product of our cumulative experiences and the interpretations we give those experiences. Hence, experience, culture and perspective are essentially one, unless we consciously separate them, and most people do not.

ROBERT STAPLES

You cannot create experience. You must undergo it.

ALBERT CAMUS

When you have really exhausted an experience you always reverence and love it.

G. K. CHESTERTON

It's all right letting yourself go, as long as you can get your-self back.

MICK JAGGER

The trouble with experience is that by the time you have it you are too old to use it.

JIMMY CONNORS

Do you know the difference between education and expe-rience? Education is when you read the fine print; experi-ence is what you get when you don't.

PETE SEEGER

Experience tells you what to do; confidence allows you to do it.

STAN SMITH

Failure

Sometimes by losing a battle you find a new way to win the war.

DONALD TRUMP

How you handle defeat is not something to be taken lightly. You've got to think it through. Defeat is an art form. You've got to accept that, and you've got to go on. And once you do that, it's not bad.

WALTER MONDALE

Once you have experienced a failure or a disappointment, once you've analyzed it and gotten the lessons out of it— dump it.

COLIN POWELL

The taste of defeat has a richness of experience all its own.

BILL BRADLEY

There is much to be said for failure. It is more interesting than success.

MAX BEERBOHM

There are two reasons why people fail. One is irresponsibility. The second is fear.

WALLY AMOS

Failures are like skinned knees—painful, but superficial.

H. ROSS PEROT

Show me a good and gracious loser and I'll show you a failure.

KNUTE ROCKNE

I don't know the key to success, but the key to failure is trying to please everybody.

BILL COSBY

Failure is only the opportunity to begin again more intelligently.

HENRY FORD

You've got to learn to survive a defeat. That's when you develop character.

RICHARD M. NIXON

Faith

How can I believe in God when just last week I got my tongue caught in the roller of an electric typewriter?

WOODY ALLEN

God not only plays dice. He also sometimes throws the dice where they cannot be seen.

STEPHEN HAWKING

With hard work, commitment and faith, there is very little that men and women of good faith cannot accomplish.

BENJAMIN HOOKS

Faith is, before all and above all, wishing God may exist.

MIGUEL DE UNAMUNO

Through faith, man experiences the meaning of the world; through action, he is to give it a meaning.

LEO BAECK

The Lord God is subtle, but malicious he is not.

ALBERT EINSTEIN

Faith means intense, usually confident, belief that is not based on evidence sufficient to command assent from every reasonable person.

WALTER KAUFMANN

We turn toward God only to obtain the impossible.

ALBERT CAMUS

Faith, to my mind, is a stiffening process, a sort of mental starch, which ought to be applied as sparingly as possible.

E. M. FORSTER

Fame

As much as you try to be a regular guy, you can't.

ROBERT REDFORD

A celebrity is someone who works hard all his life to become well known, then wears dark glasses to avoid being recognized.

FRED ALLEN

It's a short walk from hallelujah to the hoot.

VLADIMIR NABOKOV

The postman wants an autograph. The cab driver wants a picture. The waitress wants a handshake. Everyone wants a piece of you.

JOHN LENNON

If you become a star, *you* don't change, everyone else does.

KIRK DOUGLAS

A celebrity is any well-known TV or movie star who looks like he spends more than two hours working on his hair.

STEVE MARTIN

I'm real. I'm myself. Right now it's my time. One day the limelight will belong to someone else.

SHAQUILLE O'NEAL

In the future, everyone will be famous for fifteen minutes.

ANDY WARHOL

I joked about every prominent man in my lifetime, but I never met one I didn't like.

WILL ROGERS

Some are born great, some achieve greatness, and some hire public relations officers.

DANIEL J. BOORSTIN

Publicity is like poison. It doesn't hurt you unless you swallow it.

JOE PATERNO

I get a kick out of movie stars.

JACK NICHOLSON

FAMILY

Families are about love overcoming emotional torture.

MATT GROENING

The family is nature's masterpiece.

GEORGE SANTAYANA

Families break up when people take hints you don't intend
and miss hints you do intend.

ROBERT FROST

When our relatives are at home, we have to think of all their
good points or it would be impossible to endure them.

GEORGE BERNARD SHAW

Home, nowadays, is a place where part of the family waits
until the rest of the family brings the car back.

EARL WILSON

Family is a unit composed not only of children but of men,
women, an occasional animal, and the common cold.

OGDEN NASH

Families with babies and families without babies feel sorry for each other.

EDGAR WATSON HOWE

If a man has been his mother's undisputed darling he retains throughout life the triumphant feeling, the confidence in success, which not seldom brings actual success with it.

SIGMUND FREUD

A child enters your home and for the next twenty years makes so much noise you can hardly stand it. The child departs, leaving the house so silent you think you are going mad.

JOHN ANDREW HOLMES

Having a family is like having a bowling alley installed in your brain.

MARTIN MULL

Only two things are necessary to keep one's wife happy. One is to let her think she is having her own way, and the other is to let her have it.

LYNDON B. JOHNSON

To maintain a joyful family requires much from both the parents and the children. Each member of the family has to become, in a special way, the servant of the others.

POPE JOHN PAUL II

The reason grandparents and grandchildren get along so well is that they have a common enemy.

SAM LEVENSON

There is no such thing as fun for the whole family.

JERRY SEINFELD

Behind every successful man stands a surprised mother-in-law.

HUBERT HUMPHREY

Home is the place where, when you have to go there,
They have to take you in.

ROBERT FROST

A man's womenfolk, whatever their outward show of respect for his merit and authority, always regard him secretly as an ass, and with something akin to pity.

H. L. MENCKEN

The most important relationship within the family, second only to that of husband and wife, is the relationship between father and daughter.

DAVID JEREMIAH

FATHERHOOD

I felt something impossible for me to explain in words. Then when they took her away, it hit me. I got scared all over again and began to feel giddy. Then it came to me—I was a father.

NAT KING COLE

My father was frightened of his father, I was frightened of my father, and I am damned well going to see to it that my children are frightened of me.

GEORGE V, KING OF ENGLAND

But after you've raised them
and educated them and gowned them,
They just take their little fingers
and wrap you around them.

Being a father
Is quite a bother
But I like it, rather.

OGDEN NASH

I talk and talk and talk, and I haven't taught people in fifty years what my father taught me by example in one week.

MARIO CUOMO

To be a successful father there's one absolute rule: when you have a kid, don't look at it for the first two years.

ERNEST HEMINGWAY

Fatherhood is pretending the present you love the most is soap-on-a-rope.

BILL COSBY

Words have an awesome impact. The impressions made by a father's voice can set in motion an entire trend of life.

GORDON MACDONALD

By profession I am a soldier and take great pride in that fact, but I am prouder, infinitely prouder, to be a father. A soldier destroys in order to build; the father only builds, never destroys. The one has the potentialities of death; the other embodies creation and life. And while the hordes of death are mighty, the battalions of life are mightier still.

DOUGLAS MACARTHUR

Fear

The only thing we have to fear is fear itself.

FRANKLIN D. ROOSEVELT

All fear is a sign of want of faith.

MAHATMA GANDHI

Fear has the largest eyes of all.

BORIS PASTERNAK

If we take the generally accepted definition of bravery as a quality which knows no fear, I have never seen a brave man. All men are frightened. The more intelligent they are, the more they are frightened.

GEORGE S. PATTON

In acknowledging our fear, we accept our humanity.

JULIUS LESTER

Worry is prayer for something you don't want.

JAMES MITCHELL MILLER

You *have* to get beyond the fear.

DANNY GLOVER

I've only been intimidated by one thing in my life and it's not human. It's a scale.

CHARLIE KERFIELD

We must not allow fear to stand in our way. Our march to freedom is irreversible.

NELSON MANDELA

Man's loneliness is but his fear of life.

EUGENE O'NEILL

There is only one thing that a brave and honest man—a gentleman—should be afraid of. And that is death. He should carry the fear of death forever in his heart—for that ends all glory, and he should use it as a spur to ride his life across the barriers.

THOMAS WOLFE

We must travel in the direction of our fear.

JOHN BERRYMAN

FILM

The best things in movies happen by accident.

JOHN FORD

Movies have just become a kind of hallucination. An excuse to go hallucinate, like drugs. Movies are a dream world. Eat popcorn and dream.

SAM SHEPARD

Film is not to be played with. It may be our most powerful medium and should be treated as such.

SPIKE LEE

If my films make one more person miserable, I'll feel I've done my job.

WOODY ALLEN

It may be that the most avid readers of new fiction in America today are film producers, an indication of the trouble we're in.

E. L. DOCTOROW

The length of a film should be directly related to the endurance of the human bladder.

ALFRED HITCHCOCK

Movies are an art form, and twenty per cent of that art form is supplied by what the audience brings to the movie.

QUENTIN TARANTINO

An actor entering through the door, you've got nothing. But if he enters through the window, you've got a situation.

BILLY WILDER

The most expensive habit in the world is celluloid, not heroin, and I need a fix every few years.

STEVEN SPIELBERG

All Americans born between 1890 and 1945 wanted to be movie stars.

GORE VIDAL

Some films are slices of life. Mine are slices of cake.

ALFRED HITCHCOCK

The Western remains, I suppose, America's distinctive contribution to film.

ARTHUR SCHLESINGER, JR.

Nobody should come into the movies unless he believes in heroes.

JOHN WAYNE

Food

You can tell a lot about a fellow's character by his way of eating jellybeans.

RONALD REAGAN

I won't eat anything that has intelligent life but I would gladly eat a network politician.

MARTY FELDMAN

Eat as much as you like—just don't swallow it.

STEVE BURNS

We may find in the long run that tinned food is a deadlier weapon than the machine gun.

GEORGE ORWELL

Food comes first, then morals.
BERTOLT BRECHT

More die in the United States of too much food than too little.
JOHN KENNETH GALBRAITH

Old people shouldn't eat health foods. They need all the preservatives they can get.
ROBERT ORBEN

Cockroaches and socialites are the only things that can stay up all night long and eat anything.
HERB CAEN

I never see any home cooking. All I get is fancy stuff.
PRINCE PHILIP, DUKE OF EDINBURGH

I would like to find a stew that will give me heartburn immediately, instead of at three o'clock in the morning.
JOHN BARRYMORE

I'm at the age where food has taken the place of sex in my life. In fact, I've just had a mirror put over my kitchen table.
RODNEY DANGERFIELD

We didn't starve, but we didn't eat chicken unless we were sick, or the chicken was.

BERNARD MALAMUD

The first time I tried organic wheat bread, I thought I was chewing on roofing material.

ROBIN WILLIAMS

Bachelor cooking is a matter of attitude. If you think of it as setting fire to things and making a mess, it's fun. It's not so much fun if you think of it as dinner . . . Nomenclature is an important part of cooking. If you call it "Italian cheese toast," it's not disgusting to have warmed-over pizza for breakfast.

P. J. O'ROURKE

You know the rules in a cow camp when they have no regular cook? When anybody complains about the chuck, they have to do the cooking.

JOE M. EVANS

I do like a little bit of butter to my bread!

A. A. MILNE

I've known what it is to be hungry, but I always went right to a restaurant.

RING LARDNER

As a child my family's menu consisted of two choices: take it, or leave it.

BUDDY HACKETT

The secret of cooking is first, having a love of it. If you're convinced cooking is drudgery, you're never going to be any good at it, and you might as well just warm up something frozen.

JAMES BEARD

An empty stomach is not a good political advisor.

ALBERT EINSTEIN

Seeing is deceiving. It's eating that's believing.

JAMES THURBER

There are some things that sound too funny to eat . . . guacamole. That sounds like something you yell when you're on fire!

GEORGE CARLIN

There is no sincerer love than the love of food.

GEORGE BERNARD SHAW

FRIENDSHIP

My best friend is the one who brings out the best in me.

HENRY FORD

Whenever a friend succeeds, a little something in me dies.

GORE VIDAL

Some of my best friends are children. In fact, all of my best friends are children.

J. D. SALINGER

Friendship marks a life even more deeply than love. Love risks degenerating into obsession, friendship is never anything but sharing.

ELIE WIESEL

Instead of loving your enemies, treat your friends a little better.

EDGAR WATSON HOWE

If I had to choose between betraying my country and betraying my friend, I hope I should have the guts to betray my country.

E. M. FORSTER

Friends . . . are God's apology for relations.

HUGH KINGSMILL

Friendship is almost always the union of a part of one mind with part of another; people are friends in spots.

GEORGE SANTAYANA

To find a friend one must close one eye. To keep him—
two.

NORMAN DOUGLAS

Every organism requires an environment of friends, partly to
shield it from violent changes, and partly to supply it with
its wants.

ALFRED NORTH WHITEHEAD

Champagne for my real friends and real pain for my sham
friends.

TOM WAITS

I don't trust him. We're friends.

BERTOLT BRECHT

We all need someone we can bleed on.

MICK JAGGER

I get by with a little help from my friends.

JOHN LENNON AND PAUL MCCARTNEY

Friendship is the only cement that will hold the world together.

WOODROW WILSON

GENDER GAP

Women who seek to be equal with men lack ambition.

TIMOTHY LEARY

Nobody will ever win the battle of the sexes. There's too much fraternizing with the enemy.

HENRY KISSINGER

Men play the game; women know the score.

ROGER WODDIS

Men act and women appear. Men look at women. Women watch themselves being looked at.

JOHN BERGER

It is now possible for a flight attendant to get a pilot pregnant.

RICHARD J. FERRIS

The issue here is that what is often defined as sexist behavior is nothing more than men acting in ways in which they have been socialized to behave.

ROBERT STAPLES

In the past, a man was expected to give his seat to a woman. Today, it would be much more courteous for a man to give her his job.

P. J. O'ROURKE

Women will never be as successful as men because they have no wives to advise them.

DICK VAN DYKE

No longer is the female destined solely for the home and the rearing of the family and only the male for the market-place and the world of ideas.

WILLIAM J. BRENNAN

Instead of this absurd division of the sexes they ought to class people as static and dynamic.

EVELYN WAUGH

Men should be saying "I want to become a woman." The world would be a far better place if more men wanted to become women, than women wanted to become men.

ALBERT HALSEY

I prefer to call the most obnoxious feminists what they really are: feminazis.

RUSH LIMBAUGH

Without women, we stood in space on one leg only.

VLADIMIR DZANIBEKOV

The differences between the sexes are the single most important fact of human society.

GEORGE GILDER

In the sex-war, thoughtlessness is the weapon of the male, vindictiveness of the female.

CYRIL CONNOLLY

My advice to the women's clubs of America is to raise more hell and fewer dahlias.

WILLIAM ALLEN WHITE

Genius and Talent

A man of genius makes no mistakes. His errors are volitional and are the portals of discovery.

JAMES JOYCE

Whom the gods wish to destroy they first call promising.

CYRIL CONNOLLY

Talent is never enough. With a few exceptions, the best players are the hardest workers.

MAGIC JOHNSON

True genius resides in the capacity for evaluation of uncertain, hazardous, and conflicting information.

WINSTON CHURCHILL

A man possesses talent; genius possesses the man.

ISAAC STERN

There is no such thing as talent. There is pressure.

ALFRED ADLER

Unhappiness is best defined as the difference between our talents and our expectations.

EDWARD DE BONO

To exploit is not necessarily bad. To make use of someone's talent in a positive way benefits everyone.

BERRY GORDY, JR.

Genius is seldom recognized for what it is: a great capacity for hard work.

HENRY FORD

It takes a little talent to see clearly what lies under one's nose, a good deal of it to know in what direction to point that organ.

W. H. AUDEN

GOVERNMENT

Too bad all the people who know how to run the country are driving taxi cabs and cutting hair.

GEORGE BURNS

If you're hanging around with nothing to do and the zoo is closed, come over to the Senate. You'll get the same kind of feeling and you won't have to pay.

ROBERT DOLE

A government big enough to give you everything you want is big enough to take from you everything you have.

GERALD R. FORD

Any cook should be able to run the country.

VLADIMIR I. LENIN

You can fool too many of the people too much of the time.

JAMES THURBER

I find in Washington that when you ask what time it is, you get different answers from Democrats and Republicans; 435 answers from the House of Representatives; a 500-page report from some consultants on how to tell time; no answer from your lawyer and a bill for $1,000.

R. TIM MCNAMARA

A government which uses force to maintain its rule teaches the oppressed to use force to oppose it.

NELSON MANDELA

Giving money and power to the government is like giving whiskey and car keys to teenage boys.

P. J. O'ROURKE

I'm tired of people in Washington lecturing us about family values. Our families have values. The government has no values.

WILLIAM J. CLINTON

Voters don't decide issues, they decide who will decide issues.

GEORGE F. WILL

Governments never learn. Only people learn.

MILTON FRIEDMAN

GROWING UP

Grown-ups never understand anything for themselves, and it is tiresome for children to be always and forever explaining things to them.

ANTOINE DE SAINT-EXUPÉRY

When I was young there was no respect for the young, and now that I am old there is no respect for the old. I missed out coming and going.

J. B. PRIESTLEY

Definition of adolescence: A kind of emotional seasickness.

ARTHUR KOESTLER

It's a wonderful feeling when your father becomes not a god but a man to you—when he comes down from the mountain and you see he's this man with weaknesses. And you love him as this whole being, not as a figurehead.

ROBIN WILLIAMS

Each generation must out of relative obscurity discover its mission, fulfill it, or betray it.

FRANTZ FANON

The turning point in the process of growing up is when you discover the core of strength within you that survives all the hurt.

MAX LERNER

There are more bores around than when I was a boy.

FRED ALLEN

I think that for any generation to assert itself as an aware human entity, it has to break with the past, so obviously the kids that are coming along next are not going to have much in common with what we feel. They're going to create their own unique sound.

JIM MORRISON

When I grow up, I want to be a little boy.

JOSEPH HELLER

Our message: Don't grow up. Growing up means *giving up your dreams.*

JERRY RUBIN

There is always one moment in childhood when the door opens and lets the future in.

GRAHAM GREENE

If a person knew at twenty how fortunate he is to be twenty, he would get a stroke because of sheer bliss.

ARTHUR SCHNITZLER

Happiness

To be happy, we must not be too concerned with others.

ALBERT CAMUS

Happiness is your dentist telling you it won't hurt and then having him catch his hand in the drill.

JOHNNY CARSON

If all of our happiness is bound up entirely in our personal circumstances it is difficult not to demand of life more than it has to give.

BERTRAND RUSSELL

Happiness hates the timid! So does science!

EUGENE O'NEILL

We deem those happy who from the experience of life have learned to bear its ills without being overcome by them.

CARL JUNG

The bird of paradise alights only upon the hand that does not grasp.

JOHN BERRY

Happiness is the overcoming of not unknown obstacles toward a known goal.

L. RON HUBBARD

Happiness? That's nothing more than health and a poor memory.

ALBERT SCHWEITZER

Happiness is having a large, loving, caring, close-knit family in another city.

GEORGE BURNS

Happiness is a by-product.

ROBERT TRACY

Happiness makes up in height for what it lacks in length.

ROBERT FROST

HERITAGE AND HISTORY

Tradition does not mean that the living are dead; it means that the dead are living.

HAROLD MACMILLAN

Things are as they are because they were as they were.

THOMAS GOLD

If you wallow in the past, you'll stay there.

BEN VEREEN

We live in the past to an astonishing degree, the myth we live by, the presumptions we make. Nobody can look in the mirror and not see his mother or his father.

E. L. DOCTOROW

The most persistent sound which reverberates through man's history is the beating of war drums.

ARTHUR KOESTLER

More history's been made by secret handshakes than by battles, bills, and proclamations.

JOHN BARTH

History is the sum total of things that could have been avoided.

KONRAD ADENAUER

That men do not learn very much from the lessons of history is the most important of all the lessons of history.

ALDOUS HUXLEY

History is more or less bunk.

HENRY FORD

The past is a rich resource on which to draw in order to make decisions for the future, but it does not dictate our choices.

NELSON MANDELA

The cowboy spells romance in American history.

HARRY MAULE

The only time we should look back to yesterday is to look at the positive things that were accomplished to encourage us to do better things today and tomorrow.

STEVIE WONDER

I tell you the past is a bucket of ashes.

CARL SANDBURG

Heroes

Unhappy the land that is in need of heroes.

BERTOLT BRECHT

We can't all be heroes because somebody has to sit on the curb and clap as they go by.

WILL ROGERS

Ultimately a hero is a man who would argue with Gods, and so awakens devils to contest his vision.

NORMAN MAILER

We've got to examine who and what a hero is and how far we, the fans, go in putting these people up on pedestals. They're not perfect, but then again, neither are we.

BILL COSBY

The fear of God makes a hero; the fear of man makes a coward.

ALVIN YORK

Heroes may not be braver than anyone else. They're just braver five minutes longer.

RONALD REAGAN

It doesn't take a hero to order men into battle. It takes a hero to be one of those men who goes into battle.

NORMAN SCHWARZKOPF

Show me a hero and I will write you a tragedy.

F. SCOTT FITZGERALD

The ordinary man is involved in action, the hero acts. An immense difference.

HENRY MILLER

HUMAN NATURE

We are a perverse, complex people. It's what makes us lovable. We're banking heavily that God has a sense of humor.

JIM MURRAY

Most human beings have an almost infinite capacity for taking things for granted.

ALDOUS HUXLEY

Till now man has been up against Nature; from now on he will be up against his own nature.

DENNIS GABOR

When a fellow ain't got much mind, it don't take him long to make it up.

WILL ROGERS

To be human means to feel inferior.

ALFRED ADLER

There is no such thing as normality—each and every one of us, if we dare to be whole, is a gorgeous peacock.

RUPAUL

A person is a person because he recognizes others as persons.

DESMOND TUTU

There is only one basic human right, the right to do what you damn well please.

P. J. O'ROURKE

For the American people are a very generous people and will forgive almost any weakness, with the possible exception of stupidity.

WILL ROGERS

I have found little that is good about human beings. In my experience most of them are trash.

SIGMUND FREUD

We are survival machines—robot vehicles blindly programmed to preserve the selfish molecules known as genes. This is a truth which still fills me with astonishment.

RICHARD DAWKINS

The real problem is not whether machines think but whether men do.

B. F. SKINNER

The natural role of twentieth-century man is anxiety.

NORMAN MAILER

We're all just guinea pigs in the laboratory of God. Humanity is just a work in progress.

TENNESSEE WILLIAMS

I find it valid to understand man as an animal before I am prepared to know him as a man.

JOHN STEINBECK

If you hate a person, you hate something in him that is part of yourself. What isn't part of ourselves doesn't disturb us.

HERMANN HESSE

A fanatic is one who can't change his mind and won't change the subject.

WINSTON CHURCHILL

Humor

We are all here for a spell; get all the good laughs you can.

WILL ROGERS

What is comedy? Comedy is the art of making people laugh without making them puke.

STEVE MARTIN

Humor is falling downstairs if you do it while in the act of warning your wife not to.

KENNETH BIRD

You are not angry with people when you laugh at them. Humour teaches tolerance.

W. SOMERSET MAUGHAM

Jokes of the proper kind, properly told, can do more to enlighten questions of politics, philosophy, and literature than any number of dull arguments.

ISAAC ASIMOV

The funny bone is universal.

BERNARD MALAMUD

The aim of a joke is not to degrade the human being but to remind him that he is already degraded.

GEORGE ORWELL

Laughter restores the universe to its original state of indifference and strangeness: if it has a meaning, it is a divine one, not a human one.

OCTAVIO PAZ

I have seen what a laugh can do. It can transform almost unbearable tears into something bearable, even hopeful.

BOB HOPE

The whole object of comedy is to be yourself and the closer you get to that, the funnier you will be.

JERRY SEINFELD

Dig. The only honest art form is laughter, comedy. You can't fake it, Jim. Try to fake three laughs in an hour—ha ha ha ha ha—they'll take you away, man. You can't.

LENNY BRUCE

I'm a real person—life's a bitch. I live to put a smile on your face and make your life a little bit better. This is a very tough world we live in.

ARSENIO HALL

Humor can be dissected, as a frog can, but the thing dies in the process and the innards are discouraging to any but the pure scientific mind.

E. B. WHITE

In the end, everything is a gag.

CHARLIE CHAPLIN

I am kind of a paranoiac in reverse. I suspect people of plotting to make me happy.

J. D. SALINGER

Humor is emotional chaos remembered in tranquility.

JAMES THURBER

You can turn painful situations around through laughter. If you can find humor in anything—even poverty—you can survive it.

BILL COSBY

An amateur thinks it's funny if you dress a man up as an old lady, put him in a wheelchair, and give the wheelchair a push that sends it spinning down a slope towards a stone wall. For a pro, it's got to be a real old lady.

GROUCHO MARX

Everything is funny as long as it is happening to someone else.

WILL ROGERS

I love comedy. It's the only art form that's also a social grace. You meet a sculptor at a party, you can't say, "He's terrific, look what he can do with the potato salad."

PAUL REISER

Laughter is the sensation of feeling good all over, and showing it principally in one spot.

JOSH BILLINGS

Ideas

The test of a first-rate intelligence is the ability to hold two opposed ideas in the mind at the same time, and still retain the ability to function.

F. SCOTT FITZGERALD

A single idea, if it is right, saves us the labor of an infinity of experiences.

JACQUES MARITAIN

Ideas have to be wedded to action; if there is no sex, no vitality in them, there is no action. Ideas cannot exist alone in the vacuum of the mind. Ideas are related to the living.

HENRY MILLER

We are healthy only to the extent that our ideas are humane.

KURT VONNEGUT

We hold that the greatest right in the world is the right to be wrong, that in the exercise thereof people have an inviolable right to express their unbridled thoughts on all topics and personalities, being liable only for the use of that right.

WILLIAM RANDOLPH HEARST

If you want to kill an idea in the world today, get a committee working on it.

CHARLES F. KETTERING

The thinker dies, but his thoughts are beyond the reach of destruction. Men are mortal; but ideas are immortal.

WALTER LIPPMAN

Ideas move around inside people.

JOHN ZIMAN

I probably have traveled and walked into more variety stores than anybody in America. I am just trying to get ideas, any kind of ideas that will help our company. Most of us don't have ideas. We take the best ideas from someone else.

SAM WALTON

Ideas come in pairs and they contradict one another; their opposition is the principal engine of reflection.

JEAN-PAUL SARTRE

Every idea is a source of light and life which animates and illuminates the words, facts, examples, and emotions that are dead—or deadly—and dark without them.

MORTIMER J. ADLER

Nothing is so corrupting as a great idea whose time is past.

JOHN P. GRIER

ILLNESS

All interest in disease and death is only another expression of interest in life.

THOMAS MANN

Those who have never been ill are incapable of real sympathy for a great many misfortunes.

ANDRÉ GIDE

Serious illness doesn't bother me for long because I am too inhospitable a host.

ALBERT SCHWEITZER

A cough is something that you yourself can't help, but everybody else does on purpose just to torment you.

OGDEN NASH

It's no longer a question of staying healthy. It's a question of finding a sickness you like.

JACKIE MASON

The more serious the illness, the more important it is for you to fight back, mobilizing all your resources— spiritual, emotional, intellectual, physical.

NORMAN COUSINS

Use your health, even to the point of wearing it out. That is what it is for. Spend all you have before you die; and do not outlive yourself.

GEORGE BERNARD SHAW

I think we sometimes think only gay people can get it; "it's not going to happen to me." And here I am saying that it can happen to anybody, even Magic Johnson.

MAGIC JOHNSON

Imagination

Imagination is more important than knowledge.

ALBERT EINSTEIN

Imagination is not something apart and hermetic, not a way of leaving reality behind; it is a way of engaging reality.

IRVING HOWE

A man to carry on a successful business must have imagination. He must see things as in a vision, a dream of the whole thing.

CHARLES SCHWAB

Skill without imagination is craftmanship and gives us many useful objects such as wickerwork picnic baskets. Imagination without skill gives us modern art.

TOM STOPPARD

We make up horrors to help us cope with the real ones.

STEPHEN KING

The body travels more easily than the mind, and until we have limbered up our imagination we continue to think as though we had stayed home. We have not really budged a step until we take up residence in someone else's point of view.

JOHN ERSKINE

Fairyland is nothing but the sunny country of common sense.

G. K. CHESTERTON

I get the facts, I study them patiently, I apply imagination.

BERNARD BARUCH

In the world of the imagination, anything goes that's imaginatively possible, but nothing really happens.

NORTHROP FRYE

There is no victory except through our imagination.

DWIGHT D. EISENHOWER

JEALOUSY

Sex and envy are the two greatest drives in life.

LYNDON B. JOHNSON

Jealousy is the tribute mediocrity pays to genius.

FULTON J. SHEEN

It is not love that is blind, but jealousy.

LAWRENCE DURRELL

Envy is as persistent as memory, as intractable as a head cold.

HARRY STEIN

Never be possessive. If a female friend lets on that she is going out with another man, be kind and understanding. If she says that she would like to go out with all the Dallas Cowboys, including the coaching staff, the same rule applies. Tell her, "Kath, you just go right ahead and do what you feel is right." Unless you actually care for her, in which case you must see to it that she has no male contact whatsoever.

BRUCE JAY FRIEDMAN

Being with an insanely jealous person is like being in the room with a dead mammoth.

MIKE NICHOLS

Jealousy, which serves the struggle for survival, can deteriorate into the envy which draws defeat even from victory.

WILLARD GAYLIN

Envy takes the joy, happiness, and contentment out of living.

BILLY GRAHAM

JOURNALISM

An editor is one who separates the wheat from the chaff and prints the chaff.

ADLAI E. STEVENSON

Writing a column is easy. All you do every day is sit down to a typewriter, open a vein and bleed.

RED SMITH

The very blood and semen of journalism . . . is a broad and successful form of lying. Remove that form of lying and you no longer have journalism.

JAMES AGEE

A foreign correspondent is someone who lives in foreign parts and corresponds, usually in the form of essays containing no new facts. Otherwise he's someone who flies around from hotel to hotel and thinks that the most interesting thing about any story is the fact that he has arrived to cover it.

TOM STOPPARD

Freedom of the press is not an end of itself but a means to the end of a free society.

FELIX FRANKFURTER

How is the world ruled and how do wars start? Diplomats tell lies to journalists and then believe what they read.

KARL KRAUS

Rock journalism is people who can't write interviewing people who can't talk for people who can't read.

FRANK ZAPPA

Please realize that the first duty of newspapermen is to get the news and PRINT THE NEWS.

WILLIAM RANDOLPH HEARST

Journalism is the last refuge of the vaguely talented.

WALTER LIPPMANN

LANGUAGE

The American language is in a state of flux based on the survival of the unfittest.

CYRIL CONNOLLY

Nothing, surely, is more alive than a word.

J. DONALD ADAMS

Mastery of language affords remarkable power.

FRANTZ FANON

This is the sort of English up with which I will not put.

WINSTON CHURCHILL

Words are . . . awkward instruments and they will be laid aside eventually, probably sooner than we think.

WILLIAM S. BURROUGHS

Drawing on my fine command of language, I said nothing.

ROBERT BENCHLEY

Slang is language that rolls up its sleeves, spits on its hands and goes to work.

CARL SANDBURG

Semantics teaches us to watch our prejudices, and to take our exercise in other ways than jumping to conclusions. Semantics is the propagandist's worse friend.

STUART CHASE

Words are loaded pistols.

JEAN-PAUL SARTRE

A language is a dialect with an army and navy.

MAX WEINREICH

I work with language. I love the flowers of afterthought.

BERNARD MALAMUD

But if thought corrupts language, language can also corrupt thought.

GEORGE ORWELL

We shall never understand each other until we reduce the language to seven words.

KAHLIL GIBRAN

LEADERSHIP

Men fundamentally can no more get along without direction than they can without eating, drinking, or sleeping.

CHARLES DE GAULLE

Surround yourself with the best people you can find, delegate authority, and don't interfere.

RONALD REAGAN

Never tell people how to do things. Tell them what to do and they will surprise you with their ingenuity.

GEORGE S. PATTON

There are no warlike people—just warlike leaders.

RALPH BUNCHE

Be a yardstick of quality. Some people aren't used to an environment where excellence is expected.

STEPHEN JOBS

The buck stops here.

HARRY S. TRUMAN

There are times when even the best manager is like the little boy with the big dog waiting to see where the dog wants to go so he can take him there.

LEE IACOCCA

Time is neutral and does not change things. With courage and initiative, leaders change things.

JESSE JACKSON

The real leader has no need to lead—he is content to point the way.

HENRY MILLER

I want things done right. That is, I want them done my way.
FRANK ROBINSON

If an individual wants to be a leader and isn't controversial,
that means he never stood for anything.
RICHARD M. NIXON

LIBERALS

Liberal—a power worshipper without the power.
GEORGE ORWELL

For the average American, the message is clear. Liberalism
is no longer the answer. It is the problem.
RONALD REAGAN

Somehow liberals have been unable to acquire from life
what conservatives seem to be endowed with at birth:
namely, a healthy skepticism of the powers of government
agencies to do good.
DANIEL P. MOYNIHAN

A rich man told me recently that a liberal is a man who tells
other people what to do with their money.
AMIRI BARAKA (LEROI JONES)

The liberals can understand everything but people who don't understand them.

LENNY BRUCE

Hell hath no fury like a liberal scorned.

DICK GREGORY

A liberal is a man too broadminded to take his own side in a quarrel.

ROBERT FROST

LIFE LESSONS

Life is a maze in which we take the wrong turn before we have learned to walk.

CYRIL CONNOLLY

Oh, isn't life a terrible thing, thank God?

DYLAN THOMAS

Life is not a spectacle or a feast; it is a predicament.

GEORGE SANTAYANA

If life was fair, Elvis would be alive and all the impersonators would be dead.

JOHNNY CARSON

Everything has been figured out except how to live.

JEAN-PAUL SARTRE

Life is like an overlong drama through which we sit being nagged by the vague memories of having read the reviews.

JOHN UPDIKE

To understand it [life], to love it, to make it a little better, and to accept its buffetings as best we can and swim against them, knowing that we swim on and out toward a horizon we can never reach—this is all we can do.

JAMES T. FARRELL

Do not take life too seriously. You will never get out of it alive.

ELBERT HUBBARD

Life is very singularly made to surprise us (where it does not utterly appall us).

RAINER MARIA RILKE

Man is born to live and not to prepare to live.

BORIS PASTERNAK

It has long been an axiom of mine that the little things are infinitely the most important.

ARTHUR CONAN DOYLE

You can't get satisfaction living your life according to some-one else's rules.

RUPAUL

Life is just a bowl of pits.

RODNEY DANGERFIELD

I'm the one that's got to die when it's time for me to die, so let me live my life the way I want to.

JIMI HENDRIX

When you don't have any money, the problem is food. When you have money, it's sex. When you have both, it's health. If everything is simply jake, then you're frightened of death.

J. P. DONLEAVY

One day you are drinking the wine, and the next day you are picking grapes.

LOU HOLTZ

Hope for the best. Expect the worst. Life is a play. We're unrehearsed.

MEL BROOKS

Life don't run away from nobody. Life runs at people.

JOE FRAZIER

There is no cure for birth and death save to enjoy the interval.

GEORGE SANTAYANA

A man does what he must—in spite of personal consequences, in spite of obstacles and dangers and pressures—and that is the basis of all human morality.

JOHN F. KENNEDY

There is more to life than increasing its speed.

MAHATMA GANDHI

Despite the cost of living, it's still quite popular.

LAURENCE J. PETER

When life knocks you down, try to fall on your back because if you can look up, you can get up.

LES BROWN

I get up every day really humbled by the fact that there is so much that I don't know.

RON DELLUMS

Life is ten percent what you make it and ninety percent how you take it.

IRVING BERLIN

Life is what happens to you while you're busy making other plans.

JOHN LENNON

Limitations

The thing I am most aware of is my limits. And this is natural; for I never, or almost never, occupy the middle of my cage; my whole being surges toward the bars.

ANDRÉ GIDE

There are no limits on our future if we don't put limits on our people.

JACK KEMP

Limiting one's pursuits to one lone avenue without benefit of change or diversion can result in a form of vapidity which sometimes deadens the imagination.

EDWIN G. UHL

Our accepting what we are must always inhibit our being what we ought to be.

JOHN FOWLES

Our problems are man-made, therefore they may be solved by man. And man can be as big as he wants. No problem of human destiny is beyond human beings.

JOHN F. KENNEDY

Acceptance of one's life has nothing to do with resignation: it does not mean running away from the struggle. On the contrary, it means accepting it as it comes, with all the handicaps of heredity, of suffering, of psychological complexes and injustices.

PAUL TOURNIER

Knowledge of what is possible is the beginning of happiness.

GEORGE SANTAYANA

LITERATURE

Literature is the human activity that takes the fullest and most precise account of variousness, possibility, complexity, and difficulty.

LIONEL TRILLING

Great literature is simply language charged with meaning to the utmost possible degree.

EZRA POUND

The simple point is that literature belongs to the world man constructs, not to the world he sees; to his home, not his environment.

NORTHROP FRYE

Literature is mostly about having sex and not much about having children. Life is the other way around.

DAVID DODGE

All literature is gossip.

TRUMAN CAPOTE

Reality is not an inspiration for literature. At its best, literature is an inspiration for reality.

ROMAIN GARY

With both agents and publishers hungry for bestsellers, literature will have to end up a cottage industry.

ANTHONY BURGESS

Literature exists so that where one man has lived finely, ten thousand may afterwards live finely.

ARNOLD BENNETT

Literature is the art of writing something that will be read twice; journalism what will be read once.

CYRIL CONNOLLY

A man with his belly full of the classics is an enemy of the human race.

HENRY MILLER

All modern American literature comes from one book by Mark Twain called *Huckleberry Finn.*

ERNEST HEMINGWAY

Literature is news that *stays* news.

EZRA POUND

Loneliness

Life is for each man a solitary cell whose walls are mirrors.

EUGENE O'NEILL

Our trouble, as modern men, is loneliness, and this begins in the very depths of our being. No public celebration or political symphony can hope to be rid of it.

FEDERICO FELLINI

I am lonely, lonely
I was born to be lonely,
I am best so!

WILLIAM CARLOS WILLIAMS

The whole conviction of my life rests upon the belief that loneliness, far from being a rare and curious phenomenon, peculiar to myself and to a few other solitary men, is the central and inevitable fact of human existence.

THOMAS WOLFE

Our loneliness makes us avid column readers these days.

EDWARD HOAGLAND

A lonely man is a lonesome thing, a stone, a bone, a stick, a receptacle for Gilbey's gin, a stooped figure sitting at the edge of a hotel bed, heaving copious sighs like the autumn wind.

JOHN CHEEVER

If you are lonely while you are alone, you are in bad company.

JEAN-PAUL SARTRE

Loneliness is bred of a mind that has grown earth-bound.

ANTOINE DE SAINT-EXUPÉRY

Love

Never forget that the most powerful force on earth is love.

NELSON A. ROCKEFELLER

Love is not love until love's vulnerable.

THEODORE ROETHKE

I love Mickey Mouse more than any woman I've ever known.

WALT DISNEY

There's this illusion that homosexuals have sex and hetero-sexuals fall in love. That's completely untrue. Everybody wants to be loved.

BOY GEORGE

Love is just a system for getting someone to call you darling after sex.

JULIAN BARNES

If you hear bells, get your ears checked.

ERICH SEGAL

Dostoevsky said, "If there is no God, then *anything* is possible." I would say that if there is no love, *nothing* is possible. Man absolutely cannot live by himself.

ERICH FROMM

Love is the child of illusion and the parent of disillusion.

MIGUEL DE UNAMUNO

Love is only the dirty trick played on us to achieve contin-uation of the species.

W. SOMERSET MAUGHAM

In an age when the fashion is to be in love with yourself, confessing to be in love with somebody else is an admission of unfaithfulness to one's beloved.

RUSSELL BAKER

Love is many things. But more than anything it is a distur-
bance of the digestive system.

GABRIEL GARCÍA MÁRQUEZ

The meeting of two personalities is like the contact of two
chemical substances: if there is any reaction, both are trans-
formed.

CARL JUNG

Love is what you've been through with somebody.

JAMES THURBER

To fall in love is to create a religion that has a fallible god.

JORGE LUIS BORGES

Let us consider the polarity of love and hate. . . . Now, clin-
ical observation shows not only that love is with unexpected
regularity accompanied by hate (ambivalence), and not only
that in human relationships hate is frequently a forerunner
of love, but also that in many circumstances hate changes
into love and love into hate.

SIGMUND FREUD

I sold my memoirs of my love life to Parker Brothers and
they are going to make a game of it.

WOODY ALLEN

Remember, to hate, to be violent, is demeaning. It means you're afraid of the other side of the coin—to love and to be loved.

JAMES BALDWIN

True love doesn't have a happy ending; true love has no ending.

ED MCKENZIE

Luck

We must believe in luck. For how else can we explain the success of those we don't like?

JEAN COCTEAU

Luck is the residue of design.

BRANCH RICKEY

I think we consider too much the good luck of the early bird, and not enough the bad luck of the early worm.

FRANKLIN D. ROOSEVELT

Luck is opportunity meeting up with preparation, so you must prepare yourself to be lucky.

GREGORY HINES

Luck is not something you can mention in the presence of self-made men.

E. B. WHITE

The harder I work, the luckier I get.

GEORGE ALLEN

Chance is a part of reality: we are continually shaped by the forces of coincidence, the unexpected occurs with almost numbing regularity in our lives.

PAUL AUSTER

I'd rather be lucky than good.

LEFTY GOMEZ

As long as we are lucky we attribute it to our smartness; our bad luck we give the gods credit for.

JOSH BILLINGS

Marriage

Eighty percent of married men cheat in America. The rest cheat in Europe.

JACKIE MASON

Bachelors know more about women than married men. If they didn't, they'd be married too.

H. L. MENCKEN

Marriage isn't a process of prolonging the life of love, but of mummifying the corpse.

P. G. WODEHOUSE

When two people are under the influence of the most violent, most insane, most elusive, and most transient of passions, they are required to swear that they will remain in that excited, abnormal, and exhausting condition continuously until death do them part.

GEORGE BERNARD SHAW

I believe in the institution of marriage and I intend to keep trying until I get it right.

RICHARD PRYOR

I never knew what happiness was until I got married. And by then it was too late.

MAX KAUFFMAN

The best part about married life is the fights. The rest is merely so-so.

THORNTON WILDER

We sleep in separate rooms, we have dinner apart, we take separate vacations—we're doing everything we can to keep our marriage together.

RODNEY DANGERFIELD

Marriage is based on the theory that when a man discovers a brand of beer exactly to his taste he should at once throw up his job and go work in the brewery.

GEORGE JEAN NATHAN

A man can have two, maybe three love affairs while he's married. After that, it's cheating.

YVES MONTAND

I met my wife in a New York bar. We had a lot in common. We were both from California and we were both drunk.

TUG MCGRAW

Marriage is a lot like taking vitamins. It's a process that involves the supplementation of each other's minimum daily requirements.

PAUL NEWMAN

Marriage is a great institution—no family should be without it.

BOB HOPE

To keep the fire burning brightly there is one easy rule: keep the two logs together, near enough to keep each other warm and far enough apart—about a finger's breadth—for breathing room. Good fire, good marriage, same rule.

ARNOLD CROMWELL

Marriage is a bribe to make the housekeeper think she's a householder.

THORNTON WILDER

We've been married twenty-eight years, and we still go out dining and dancing three times a week. She goes on Mondays, Wednesdays, and Fridays; I go on Tuesdays, Thursdays, and Saturdays.

TOMMY LASORDA

Marriage is like a bank account. You put it in, you take it out, you lose interest.

IRWIN COREY

Media

All I've been asked by the press . . . is about a woman I didn't sleep with and a draft I didn't dodge.

WILLIAM J. CLINTON

I always turn to the sports page first. The sports page records people's accomplishments; the front page nothing but man's failure.

EARL WARREN

It's the responsibility of the media to look at the president with a microscope, but they go too far when they use a proctoscope.

RICHARD M. NIXON

The one function that TV news performs very well is that when there is no news we give it to you with the same emphasis as if there were.

DAVID BRINKLEY

I never give interviews because I have no views to inter.

SAMUEL BECKETT

What the mass media offer is not popular art, but entertainment which is intended to be consumed like food, forgotten and replaced by a new dish.

W. H. AUDEN

You furnish the pictures and I'll furnish the war.

WILLIAM RANDOLPH HEARST

In dealing with the press, do yourself a favor. Stick with one of three responses: (a) I know and I can tell you, (b) I know and I can't tell you, or (c) I don't know.

DAN RATHER

In the United States there is no phenomenon more threatening to popular government than the unwillingness of newspapers to give the facts to their readers.

NELSON ANTRIM CRAWFORD

Media is just a word that means bad journalism.

GRAHAM GREENE

The function of the press is very high. It is almost holy. To misstate or suppress the news is a breach of trust.

LOUIS D. BRANDEIS

Whatever else can be said for or against our national media, their attention span is short: and so public life moves on.

HENRY HYDE

The medium is the message.

MARSHALL MCLUHAN

If it weren't for bad news, we wouldn't have any news at all.

JAMES R. PETERSON

I can remember a reporter asking me for a quote, and I didn't know what a quote was. I thought it was some kind of soft drink.

JOE DIMAGGIO

MEMORY

You lose your immortality when you lose your memory.

VLADIMIR NABOKOV

Human memory works its own wheel, and stops where it will, entirely without reference to the last stop, and with no connection to the next.

WILLIAM SAROYAN

A bad conscience has a good memory.

H. G. WELLS

The heart's memory eliminates the bad and magnifies the good; and thanks to this artifice we manage to endure the burdens of the past.

GABRIEL GARCÍA MÁRQUEZ

A retentive memory may be a good thing, but the ability to forget is the true token of greatness.

ELBERT HUBBARD

Our memories are card indexes consulted, and then put back in disorder by authorities we do not control.

CYRIL CONNOLLY

Memories are like mulligatawny soup in a cheap restaurant. It is best not to stir them.

P. G. WODEHOUSE

Even memory is not necessary for love. There is the land of the living and a land of the dead and the bridge is love, the only survival, the only meaning.

THORNTON WILDER

God created memory so that we might have roses in December.

ITALO SVEVO

Men on Women

Women are just like cats. To win them, you must first make them purr.

SAM (SULLY) GEHRING

I believe a little incompatibility is the spice of life, particularly if he has income and she is pattable.

OGDEN NASH

One of the incredible things about women is that they have the capacity to experience and to feel so much more. And that they are just so magnificent.

DANNY GLOVER

Women like silent men. They think they're listening.

MARCEL ACHARD

I'm not afraid to show my feminine side—it's part of what makes me a man.

GÉRARD DEPARDIEU

I've always wanted to be Brigitte Bardot.

BOB DYLAN

When in this world a man comes forward with a thought, a deed, a vision, we ask not how does he look, but what is his message? . . . The world still wants to ask that a woman primarily be pretty.

W. E. B. DU BOIS

I have come here to ask your help. There's an old Irish saying, "Never send a boy to do a man's job—send a lady!"

JOHN F. KENNEDY

Anyone who says he can see through women is missing a lot.

GROUCHO MARX

Women are smarter than men because they listen.

PHIL DONAHUE

Women have more imagination than men. They need it to tell us how wonderful we are.

ARNOLD GLASOW

To enter life by way of the vagina is as good a way as any.

HENRY MILLER

It was a blonde, a blonde to make a bishop kick a hole in a stained glass window.

RAYMOND CHANDLER

That's the thing about girls. Every time they do something pretty, even if they're not much to look at, or even if they're sort of stupid, you fall half in love with them, and then you never know *where* the hell you are. Girls. Jesus Christ. They can drive you crazy. They really can.

J. D. SALINGER

There's a great woman behind every idiot.

JOHN LENNON

The great question . . . which I have not been able to answer, despite my thirty years of research into the feminine soul, is "What does a woman want?"

SIGMUND FREUD

A lady is nothing very specific. One man's lady is another man's woman; sometimes, one man's lady is another man's wife. Definitions overlap but they almost never coincide.

RUSSELL LYNES

'Twas a woman who drove me to drink, and I never had the courtesy to thank her for it.

W. C. FIELDS

I like a woman with a head on her shoulders. I hate necks.

STEVE MARTIN

To call women the weaker sex is a libel: it is man's injustice to woman. If by strength is meant brute strength, then indeed, is woman less brute than man. If by strength is meant moral power, then woman is immeasurably man's superior. Has she not greater intuition, is she not more self-sacrificing, has she not greater powers of endurance, has she not greater courage? Without her, man would not be. If non-violence is the law of our being, the future is with women.

MAHATMA GANDHI

Mistakes

A life spent making mistakes is not only more honorable but more useful than a life spent doing nothing.

GEORGE BERNARD SHAW

I don't want to make the wrong mistake.

YOGI BERRA

If we had more time for discussion we should probably have made a great many more mistakes.

LEON TROTSKY

Honey, I just forgot to duck.

JACK DEMPSEY

If only one could have two lives: the first in which to make one's mistakes, which seem as if they have been made; and the second in which to profit by them.

D. H. LAWRENCE

When I make a mistake, it's a beaut!

FIORELLO LA GUARDIA

I zigged when I should have zagged.

JACK ROPER

I've made mistakes in my life. But God knows I've never been at a loss for a solution, even when it was wrong. A good general always has another plan.

JOHN H. JOHNSON

If I wasn't making mistakes, I wasn't making decisions.

ROBERT W. JOHNSON

If you don't learn from your mistakes, someone else will.

BRUCE LANSKY AND K. L. JONES

Money

Security is the only thing I want. Money to do nothing with, money to have in case you want to do something.

PAUL MCCARTNEY

My problem lies in reconciling my gross habits with my net income.

ERROL FLYNN

Money brings a certain happiness, but after a certain point, it just brings more money.

NEIL SIMON

I was brought up to believe the important thing was not how much money you want but how much money you save.

GRANT HILL

You can be young without money but you can't be old without it.

TENNESSEE WILLIAMS

I measure it by Cadillacs. I used to pay $5,000 for mine. They pay $20,000 now. So, if they make three times as much as I did, what's the difference.

MICKEY MANTLE

I have one basic drive on my side they can't defeat—greed.

FRANK ZAPPA

Money is better than poverty, if only for financial reasons.

WOODY ALLEN

I learned ages ago that money cannot make you happy. And I realized that unless you have money, you can't make a statement.

BERRY GORDY, JR.

No one can earn a million dollars honestly.

WILLIAM JENNINGS BRYAN

A billion here, a billion there—pretty soon it adds up to real money.

EVERETT DIRKSON

Money, it turned out, was exactly like sex; you thought of nothing else if you didn't have it and thought of other things if you did.

JAMES BALDWIN

I have enough money to last me the rest of my life, unless
I buy something.

JACKIE MASON

I like to walk about admist the beautiful things that adorn
the world; but private wealth I should decline, or any sort
of personal possessions, because they would take away my
liberty.

GEORGE SANTAYANA

There is nothing wrong with men possessing riches but the
wrong comes when riches possess men.

BILLY GRAHAM

Man cannot live by profit alone.

JAMES BALDWIN

Music

The only way that people will be able to see a picture of
unity is through music, through dance and rhythms coming
together.

STEVIE WONDER

Rap is the CNN of the streets.

GERALD M. LEVIN

My music is best understood by children and animals.

IGOR STRAVINSKY

Most people get into bands for three very simple rock and roll reasons: to get laid, to get fame, and to get rich.

BOB GELDOF

Life can't be all bad when for ten dollars you can buy all the Beethoven sonatas and listen to them for ten years.

WILLIAM F. BUCKLEY, JR.

Music and silence . . . combine strongly because music is done with silence, and silence is full of music.

MARCEL MARCEAU

If you have to ask what jazz is, you'll never know.

LOUIS ARMSTRONG

I was in love with rock 'n' roll because rock does this thing to you. You get directly to somebody, unfiltered.

LOU REED

Opera is when a guy gets stabbed in the back and, instead of bleeding, he sings.

ED GARDNER

Motown was a world unto itself—and the sound was a benefit of that kind of world.

BERRY GORDY, JR.

Commercial rock 'n' roll music is a brutalization of the stream of contemporary Negro church music . . . an obscene looting of a cultural expression.

RALPH ELLISON

Jazz will endure just as long as people hear it through their feet instead of their brains.

JOHN PHILIP SOUSA

I don't know anything about music. In my line you don't have to.

ELVIS PRESLEY

I like to feel that I can play many styles of music. And I play it because I enjoy it, and it's alright with me if they call it the blues.

B. B. KING

I was born with music in me.

RAY CHARLES

I have a sweet tooth for song and music. This is my Polish sin.

POPE JOHN PAUL II

To me music is always just love, I guess, just happiness. Singin' a happy song. I don't think politics should enter into music. When it does, it makes me a little queasy. 'Cause I don't dig politics that much.

MARTY BALIN

I said years and years ago, "Why play Beethoven when you can start something new?"

MILES DAVIS

I hate music, especially when it's played.

JIMMY DURANTE

It seems obvious that painting, sculpture or drama imitated nature. But what does music imitate? The measurements suggest that music is imitating the characteristic way our world changes in time.

RICHARD FREDERICK VOSS

Optimism

Gray skies are just clouds passing over.

DUKE ELLINGTON

It ain't as bad as you think. It will look better in the morning.

COLIN POWELL

If I didn't have spiritual faith, I would be a pessimist. But I'm an optimist. I've read the last page in the Bible. It's all going to turn out all right.

BILLY GRAHAM

I have discovered in life that there are ways of getting almost anywhere you want to go, if you really want to go.

LANGSTON HUGHES

If we never had any storms, we couldn't appreciate the sunshine.

DALE EVANS

We must accept finite disappointment, but we must never lose infinite hope.

MARTIN LUTHER KING, JR.

When you are looking for obstacles, you can't find opportunities.

J. C. BELL

Optimism is the content of small men in high places.

F. SCOTT FITZGERALD

I always tried to turn every disaster into an opportunity.

JOHN D. ROCKEFELLER

Tomorrow comes to us at midnight very clean. It's perfect when it arrives, and it puts itself in our hands and hopes we've learnt something from yesterday.

JOHN WAYNE

Parents

Parents are sometimes a disappointment to their children. They don't fulfill the promise of their early years.

ANTHONY POWELL

If parents would only realize how they bore their children.

GEORGE BERNARD SHAW

There are only two kinds of parents. Those who think their offspring can do nothing wrong, and those who think they can do nothing right.

MILES FRANKLIN

Parents are not quite interested in justice. They are interested in quiet.

BILL COSBY

Believe me, when I was five years old I could read my ABCs. I could count before I could even go to school. Guess who I got it from? My mother.

RAY CHARLES

Parents are the bones on which children sharpen their teeth.

PETER USTINOV

I have found the best way to give advice to your children is to find out what they want to do and then advise them to do it.

HARRY S. TRUMAN

Parents who expect gratitude from their children (there are some who even insist on it) are like usurers who gladly risk their capital if only they receive interest.

FRANZ KAFKA

There are times when parenthood seems nothing but feeding the mouth that bites you.

PETER DE VRIES

He is too experienced a parent ever to make positive promises.

CHRISTOPHER MORLEY

The pressures of being a parent are equal to any pressure on earth. To be a conscious parent, and really look to the little being's mental and physical health, is a responsibility which most of us, including me, avoid most of the time because it's too hard.

JOHN LENNON

The first half of our lives is ruined by our parents, and the second half by our children.

CLARENCE S. DARROW

She climbed into my lap and curled into the crook of my left arm. I couldn't move that arm, but I could cradle Ashtin in it. I could kiss the top of her head. And I could have no doubt that this was one of the sweetest moments of my life.

DENNIS BYRD

PATRIOTISM

Patriotism is a pernicious, psychopathic form of idiocy.

GEORGE BERNARD SHAW

True patriotism hates injustice in its own land more than anywhere else.

CLARENCE S. DARROW

I feel that this do-or-die, my-country-right-or-wrong kind of patriotism is not merely out of place in a nuclear armed world, it is criminal egotism on a monstrous scale. The world won't be safe until people in all countries recognize it for what it is and, instead of cheering the leader who talks that way, impeach him.

DR. BENJAMIN SPOCK

Patriotism is the veneration of real estate above principles.

GEORGE JEAN NATHAN

Americanism is a question of principle, of idealism, of character: it is not a matter of birthplace or creed or line of descent.

THEODORE ROOSEVELT

I drink beer, I swear and I keep my hair short, so I guess you'd call me an All-American boy.

TOM SEAVER

Patriotism is your conviction that this country is superior to all other countries because you were born in it.

GEORGE BERNARD SHAW

Nations whose nationalism is destroyed are subject to ruin.

MUAMMAR AL-QADDAFI

Patriotism, to be truly American, begins with the human allegiance.

NORMAN COUSINS

It is a very dangerous thing to organize the patriotism of a nation if you are not sincere.

ERNEST HEMINGWAY

Patriotism is not short, frenzied outbursts of emotion, but the tranquil and steady devotion of a lifetime.

ADLAI E. STEVENSON

Pets

I have a rock garden. Last week three of them died.

RICHARD DIRAN

I don't know what the cat can have eaten. Usually I know exactly what the cat has eaten. Not only have I fed it to the cat, at the cat's keen insistence, but the cat has thrown it up on the rug and someone has tracked it all the way over onto the other rug. I don't know why cats are such habitual vomiters. They don't seem to enjoy it, judging by the sounds they make while doing it. It's in their nature. A dog is going to bark. A cat is going to vomit.

ROY BLOUNT, JR.

I take my pet lion to church every Sunday. He has to eat.

MARTY POLLILO

The best thing about animals is that they don't talk much.

THORNTON WILDER

Cats are intended to teach us that not everything in nature has a function.

GARRISON KEILLOR

A dog teaches a boy fidelity, perseverance, and to turn around three times before lying down.

ROBERT BENCHLEY

Poetry

But all art is sensual and poetry particularly so. It is directed, that is, of the senses, and since the senses do not exist without an object for their employment all art is necessarily objective. It doesn't declaim or explain, it presents.

WILLIAM CARLOS WILLIAMS

The crown of literature is poetry. It is its end and aim. It is the sublimest activity of the human mind. It is the achievement of beauty and delicacy. The writer of prose can only step outside when the poet passes.

W. SOMERSET MAUGHAM

The greatest poem ever known
Is one all poets have outgrown:
The poetry, innate, untold,
Of being four years old.

CHRISTOPHER MORLEY

A poem should not mean
But be.

ARCHIBALD MACLEISH

Poetry lies its way to the truth.

JOHN CIARDI

In one sense the efficacy of poetry is nil—no lyric has ever stopped a tank. In another sense, it is unlimited. It is like writing in the sand in the face of which accusers and accused are left speechless.

SEAMUS HEANEY

There is no money in poetry, but then there is no poetry in money either.

ROBERT GRAVES

Poetry is the achievement of the synthesis of hyacinths and biscuits.

CARL SANDBURG

Poetry makes nothing happen: it survives
In the valley of its saying.

W. H. AUDEN

Poetry is to prose as dancing is to walking.

JOHN WAIN

Poetry is a way of taking life by the throat.

ROBERT FROST

Poetry must be *as well written as prose.*

EZRA POUND

Poetry is an orphan of silence. The words never quite equal
the experience behind them.

CHARLES SIMIC

Poets

A poet is not a public figure. A poet should be read and not
seen.

C. DAY LEWIS

The writing of more than 75 poems in any fiscal year should
be punishable by a fine of $500.

ED SANDERS

There is no advice to give young poets.

PABLO NERUDA

Immature poets imitate; mature poets steal.

T. S. ELIOT

Deprivation is for me what daffodils were to Wordsworth.

PHILIP LARKIN

I'd rather be a great bad poet than a bad good poet.

OGDEN NASH

Pitchers, like poets, are born not made.

CY YOUNG

I am not feeling very well. I can only write prose today.

WILLIAM BUTLER YEATS

We all write poems; it is simply that poets are the ones who write in words.

JOHN FOWLES

Politics

Politics is the best show in America. I love animals and I love politicians and I love to watch both of 'em play, either back home in their native state or after they have been captured and sent to the zoo or to Washington.

WILL ROGERS

Too bad ninety percent of the politicians give the other ten percent a bad reputation.

HENRY KISSINGER

All politics is local.

THOMAS P. "TIP" O'NEILL

It is not true that only coldhearted, cynical, arrogant, haughty or brawling persons can succeed in politics. Such people are naturally attracted by politics. In the end, however, politeness and good manners weigh more.

VÁCLAV HAVEL

Being in politics is like being a football coach. You have to be smart enough to understand the game and stupid enough to think it's important.

EUGENE MCCARTHY

Politicians are the same all over. They promise to build bridges, even where there are no rivers.

NIKITA KHRUSHCHEV

I have only one firm belief about the American political system, and that is this: God is a Republican and Santa Claus is a Democrat.

P. J. O'ROURKE

Politics is supposed to be the second oldest profession. I have come to realize that it bears a very close relationship to the first.

RONALD REAGAN

Public life is regarded as the crown of a career, and to young men it is the worthiest ambition. Politics is still the greatest and the most honorable adventure.

JOHN BUCHAN

After all, what does a politician have but his credibility?

SPIRO T. AGNEW

Politics are about as exciting as war and quite as dangerous. In war you can only be killed once, but in politics many times.

WINSTON CHURCHILL

In football, the enemy had numbers on and were out in front where you could see them. That's not always the case in politics.

JACK KEMP

Republicans raise dahlias, Dalmatians, and eyebrows. Democrats raise Airedales, kids, and taxes.

WILL STANTON

Politics is war without bloodshed while war is politics with bloodshed.

MAO TSE-TUNG

All political ideas cannot and should not be channeled into the programs of our two major parties. History has amply proved the virtue of political activity by minority, dissident groups, who innumerable times have been the vanguard of democratic thought and whose programs were ultimately accepted.

EARL WARREN

Politics, of course, requires sweat, work, combat, and organization. But these should not be ugly words for any free people.

NELSON A. ROCKEFELLER

Power

Power corrupts, but lack of power corrupts absolutely.

ADLAI E. STEVENSON

The lust for power is not rooted in strength, but in weakness.

ERICH FROMM

We have, I fear, confused power with greatness.

STEWART UDALL

Power is inflicting pain and humiliation. Power is in tearing human minds to pieces and putting them together again in new shapes of our own choosing.

GEORGE ORWELL

Power corrupts, but absolute power is really neat.

JOHN LEHMAN

Power recognizes only power, and all of them who realize this have made gains.

MALCOLM X

As a matter of fact and experience, the more power is divided the more irresponsible it becomes.

WOODROW WILSON

Much good can come from the prudent use of power.

GEORGE BUSH

Those carried away by power are soon carried away.

MALCOLM FORBES

Power is the great aphrodisiac.

HENRY KISSINGER

Prejudice

Most men, when they think they are thinking, are merely rearranging their prejudices.

KNUTE ROCKNE

The most potent weapon in the hands of the oppressor is the mind of the oppressed.

STEVE BILKO

I am free of all prejudices. I hate everyone equally.

W. C. FIELDS

Black people can't be racist. Racism is an institution.

SPIKE LEE

Common sense is the collection of prejudices acquired by age eighteen.

ALBERT EINSTEIN

Injustice anywhere is a threat to justice everywhere.

MARTIN LUTHER KING, JR.

Everyone is a prisoner of his own experiences. No one can eliminate prejudices—just recognize them.

EDWARD R. MURROW

I hang onto my prejudices, they are the testicles of my mind.

ERIC HOFFER

Prejudice is a raft onto which the shipwrecked mind clambers and paddles to safety.

BEN HECHT

Bias and prejudice are attitudes to be kept in hand, not attitudes to be avoided.

CHARLES CURTIS

You can't hold a man down without staying down with him.

BOOKER T. WASHINGTON

Presidency

When I was a boy I was told that anyone could be president. I'm beginning to believe it.

CLARENCE S. DARROW

A president's hardest task is not to do what's right, but to know what's right.

LYNDON B. JOHNSON

I do not choose to run for President in nineteen twenty-eight.

CALVIN COOLIDGE

The thought of being President frightens me and I do not think I want the job.

RONALD REAGAN

I am a Ford, not a Lincoln. My addresses will never be as eloquent as Lincoln's. But I will do my best to equal his brevity and plain speaking.

GERALD R. FORD

I just received the following wire from my generous Daddy [Joseph P. Kennedy]—"Dear Jack. Don't buy a single vote more than necessary. I'll be damned if I'm going to pay for a landslide."

JOHN F. KENNEDY

When the President does it, that means it is not illegal.

RICHARD M. NIXON

Anybody that wants the presidency so much that he'll spend two years organizing and campaigning for it is not to be trusted with the office.

DAVID BRODER

I'm Jimmy Carter, and I'm going to be your next President.

JIMMY CARTER

You know how it is in an election year. They pick a president and then for four years they pick on him.

ADLAI E. STEVENSON

All the President is, is a glorified public relations man who spends his time flattering, kissing and kicking people to get them to do what they are supposed to do anyway.

HARRY S. TRUMAN

I'm not sure I've even got the brains to be President.

BARRY GOLDWATER

I can think of nothing more boring for the American people than to have to sit in their living rooms for a whole half hour looking at my face on their television screens.

DWIGHT D. EISENHOWER

The office of the President is such a bastardized thing, half royalty and half democracy, that nobody knows whether to genuflect or spit.

JIMMY BRESLIN

RACE

Being black is too emotionally taxing; therefore, I will be black only on weekends and holidays.

GEORGE C. WOLFE

I realize that I'm black, but I like to be viewed as a person, and that's everybody's wish.

MICHAEL JORDAN

It isn't a matter of black is beautiful as much as it is white is not *all* that's beautiful.

BILL COSBY

I was so excited when I came North and sat in the front of the bus, that I missed my stop.

DICK GREGORY

Let [racism] be a problem to someone else. . . . Let it drag them down. Don't use it as an excuse for your own short-comings.

COLIN POWELL

I want every American free to stand up for his rights, even if he has to sit down for them.

JOHN F. KENNEDY

The world is white no longer, and it will never be white again.

JAMES BALDWIN

I'd rather be black than gay because when you're black you don't have to tell your mother.

CHARLES PIERCE

There are very few perceptions in this country that are not tinged by race.

BRYANT GUMBEL

When you are fighting for justice and democracy, color, race, and social class have little importance. . . . Man taken in his totality transcends questions of race.

JEAN-BERTRAND ARISTIDE

I have a dream that my four little children will one day live in a nation where they will not be judged by the color of their skin, but by the content of their character.

MARTIN LUTHER KING, JR.

Damn the money. Damn the heavyweight championship. Damn the white people. Damn everything. I will die before I sell out my people for the white man's money.

MUHAMMAD ALI

The black man who wants to turn his race white is as miserable as he who preaches hatred for the whites.

FRANTZ FANON

My great-grandfather . . . was the first Black political candidate in the state of Mississippi. He ran for the border and made it. And the reason he ran for the border, he said, was that the people were very clannish. He didn't mind them having hang-ups, he just didn't want to be one of their hang-ups.

REDD FOXX

The burden of being black is that you have to be superior just to be equal. But the glory of it is that, once you achieve, you have achieved, indeed.

JESSE JACKSON

You show me a black man who isn't an extremist and I'll show you one who needs psychiatric attention.

MALCOLM X

I don't want to take anything away from Dr. [Martin Luther] King. He was a close personal friend of mine. But through baseball, Jackie [Robinson] did more to tear down segregation, [in] hotels and sports arenas than any other man. Nobody will ever do more, because it won't ever be necessary again.

DON NEWCOMBER

Reading

Have you ever tried neuroxing papers? It's a very easy and cheap process. You hold the page in front of your eyes and you let it go through there into the brain. It's much better than xeroxing.

SYDNEY BRENNER

Where do I find the time for not reading so many books?

KARL KRAUS

There are two motives for reading a book: one, that you enjoy it, the other that you can boast about it.

BERTRAND RUSSELL

Reading made Don Quixote a gentleman, but believing what he read made him mad.

GEORGE BERNARD SHAW

I took a speed reading course and was able to read *War and Peace* in twenty minutes. It's about Russia.

WOODY ALLEN

I would sooner read a timetable or a catalogue than nothing at all.

W. SOMERSET MAUGHAM

Reading, to most people, means an ashamed way of killing time disguised under a dignified name.

ERNEST DIMNET

We shouldn't teach great books; we should teach a love of reading.

B. F. SKINNER

I'm quite illiterate, but I read a lot.

J. D. SALINGER

I read to entertain myself, to educate myself, as a way to enlighten myself—as a way to challenge my beliefs about myself.

LEVAR BURTON

People say life is the thing, but I prefer reading.

LOGAN PEARSALL SMITH

REALITY

Each person paints their picture of reality with a brush dipped in the pigments of the past.

JERRY ANDRUS

Humankind cannot bear very much reality.

T. S. ELIOT

I know I missed stuff. But I don't know exactly what. For most of my life I never lived in the real world.

KAREEM ABDUL-JABBAR

I have lived long enough to be battered by the realities of life and not too long to be drowned by them.

JOHN MASON BROWN

Reality is a staircase going neither up nor down, we don't move, today is today, always is today.

OCTAVIO PAZ

The grass may look greener on the other side of the fence, but it's just as hard to cut.

LITTLE RICHARD

Life is washed in the speechless past.

JACQUES BARZUN

Reality must take precedence over public relations, for nature cannot be fooled.

RICHARD FEYNMAN

We should face reality and our past mistakes in an honest, adult way. Boasting of glory does not make glory, and singing in the dark does not dispel fear.

HUSSEIN, KING OF JORDAN

If men refuse to change the practice of reality to make the dream a reality and keep on sleeping on reality, hoping for a doctor, this generation will pass and another will come and they'll face the same problems that we faced.

LOUIS FARRAKHAN

It helps to see the actual world to visualize a fantastic world.

WALLACE STEVENS

REGRETS

Once a decision was made, I did not worry about it afterward.

HARRY S. TRUMAN

Never worry about anything that is past. Charge it up to experience and forget the trouble. There are always plenty of troubles ahead, so don't turn and look back on any behind you.

HERBERT HOOVER

My one regret in life is that I am not someone else.

WOODY ALLEN

Let us not bankrupt our todays by paying interest on the regrets of yesterday and by borrowing in advance the troubles of tomorrow.

RALPH W. SOCKMAN

"Henry," I said, "we've done it." I said: "Remember Lot's wife. Never look back." I don't know if Henry [Kissinger] had read the Old Testament or not, but I had, and he got the point. Henry and I often had a little joke between us after that. Whenever he would come in and say, "Well, I'm not sure we should have done this, or that, or the other thing," I would say, "Henry, remember Lot's wife." And that would end the conversation.

RICHARD M. NIXON

Regrets and recriminations only hurt your soul.

ARMAND HAMMER

Regret is an odd emotion becomes it comes only upon reflection. Regret lacks immediacy, and so its power seldom influences events when it could do some good.

WILLIAM O'ROURKE

Relationships

There is no hope of joy except in human relations.

ANTOINE DE SAINT-EXUPÉRY

What people don't realize is that intimacy has its conventions as well as ordinary social intercourse. There are three cardinal rules—don't take somebody else's boyfriend unless you've been specifically invited to do so, don't take a drink without being asked, and keep a scrupulous accounting in financial matters.

W. H. AUDEN

The bonds that unite another person to oneself exist only in our mind.

MARCEL PROUST

She was a lovely girl. Our courtship was fast and furious—I was fast and she was furious.

MAX KAUFFMAN

All couples must bear the strain of getting acquainted, having been, up to then, merely intimate.

PETER DE VRIES

The bravest thing men do is love women.

MORT SAHL

If men knew all that women think, they'd be twenty times more daring.

ALPHONSE KARR

We can't all be friends and relatives as the world is; most of us have to be strangers.

BERNARD MALAMUD

Religion

What mean and cruel things men do for the love of God.

W. SOMERSET MAUGHAM

The history of saints is mainly the history of insane people.

BENITO MUSSOLINI

One man's theology is another man's belly laugh.

ROBERT A. HEINLEIN

The Bible must be put away in libraries where it belongs. Filed to gather dust beneath appropriate labels: Mythology, Ancient History, Superstition, Folk-lore, Pre-scientific Philosophy, and so on.

PHILIP WYLIE

Science is the religion of the suburbs.

WILLIAM BUTLER YEATS

I do benefits for all religions—I'd hate to blow the hereafter
on a technicality.

BOB HOPE

Religions are such stuff as dreams are made of.

H. G. WELLS

The hardest thing for me to believe about the Bible is that
there were only two asses on Noah's Ark.

LARRY WILDE

Religion has lost itself in cults, dogmas, and myths. Con-
sequently the office of religion as a sense of community and
one's place in it has been lost.

JOHN DEWEY

Every day people are straying away from the church and
going back to God.

LENNY BRUCE

Get rid of the devil and the priest will have nothing to do.

NIKITA KHRUSHCHEV

All your Western theologies, the whole mythology of them, are based on the concept of God as a senile delinquent.

TENNESSEE WILLIAMS

I have spent a lot of time searching through the Bible for loopholes.

W. C. FIELDS

I don't like religion much, and I am glad that in the Bible the word is not to be found.

MARTIN BUBER

I believe in the fundamental Truth of all the great religions of the world. I believe that they are all God given. . . . I came to the conclusion long ago . . . that all religions were true, and also that all had some error in them.

MAHATMA GANDHI

Religions change; beer and wine remain.

HERVEY ALLEN

The Self

One may understand the cosmos, but never the ego; the self is more distant than any star.

G. K. CHESTERTON

There will be those who will tell you, you can't make it because of where you live, because of how you look, because of the way you talk. We all have heard that. . . . I almost listened.

L. DOUGLAS WILDER

To be a great champion you must believe you are the best. If you're not, pretend you are.

MUHAMMAD ALI

What we must decide is perhaps how we are valuable, rather than how valuable we are.

F. SCOTT FITZGERALD

The self is not something ready-made, but something in continuous formation through choice of action.

JOHN DEWEY

If you don't love yourself, you have nothing to hold on to.

BEN VEREEN

Character is an essential tendency. It can be covered up, it can be messed with, it can be screwed around with, but it can't be ultimately changed. It's like the structure of our bones, the blood that runs through our veins.

SAM SHEPARD

Uniformity and freedom are incompatible. Uniformity and mental health are incompatible.

ERICH FROMM

We are all serving a life-sentence in the dungeon of the self.

CYRIL CONNOLLY

I have always tried to be true to myself, to pick those battles I felt were important. My ultimate responsibility is to myself. I could never be anything else.

ARTHUR ASHE

Without being and remaining oneself, there is no love.

MARTIN BUBER

I am not going to change who I am to please anybody.

GRANT HILL

Sex

The good thing about masturbation is that you don't have to dress up to do it.

TRUMAN CAPOTE

There is hardly anyone whose sexual life, if it were broadcast, would not fill the world at large with surprise and horror.

W. SOMERSET MAUGHAM

Sex is one of the nine reasons for re-incarnation. . . . The other eight are unimportant.

HENRY MILLER

The only unnatural sex act is that which you cannot perform.

ALFRED KINSEY

What I like about masturbation is that you don't have to talk afterwards.

MILOS FORMAN

Sex is the biggest nothing of all time.

ANDY WARHOL

Life without sex might be safer but it would be unbearably dull. It is the sex instinct which makes women seem beautiful, which they are once in a blue moon, and men seem wise and brave, which they never are at all. Throttle it, denaturalize it, take it away, and human existence would be reduced to the prosaic, laborious, boresome, imbecile level of life in an anthill.

H. L. MENCKEN

If God had meant us to have group sex, he'd have given us more organs.

MALCOLM BRADBURY

Sex is good, but not as good as fresh sweet corn.

GARRISON KEILLOR

One has to be extraordinarily lucky, in our society, to meet one nymphomaniac in a lifetime.

ALEX COMFORT

By nature, I am not monogamous.

JACK NICHOLSON

You gotta learn that if you don't get it by midnight, chances are you ain't gonna get it, and if you do, it ain't worth it.

CASEY STENGEL

Masturbation! The amazing availability of it!

JAMES JOYCE

Everything takes longer than it should, with the possible exception of sex.

JIM MCGINN

Sexual Attraction

Why did [God] give us genitals then if he wanted us to think clearly?

GRAHAM GREENE

When turkeys mate, they think of swans.
JOHNNY CARSON

I'm too shy to express my sexual needs except over the phone to people I don't know.
GARRY SHANDLING

I'll tell you something
I think you'll understand,
Then I'll say that something,
I want to hold your hand.
JOHN LENNON AND PAUL MCCARTNEY

It is no longer enough to be lusty. One must be a sexual gourmet.
GEORGE F. WILL

So many beautiful women and so little time.
JOHN BARRYMORE

I can't understand why more people aren't bisexual. It would double your chances for a date Saturday night.
WOODY ALLEN

What most men desire is a virgin who is a whore.
EDWARD DAHLBERG

Girls are always running through my mind. They don't dare walk.

ANDY GIBB

My attitude toward anybody's sexual persuasion is this: without deviation from the norm, progress is not possible.

FRANK ZAPPA

I wasn't kissing her, I was whispering in her mouth.

CHICO MARX

Last time I made love to my wife nothing was happening, so I said to her: "What's the matter? You can't think of anybody either?"

RODNEY DANGERFIELD

I kissed my first girl and smoked my first cigarette on the same day. I haven't had time for tobacco since.

ARTURO TOSCANINI

I've looked on a lot of women with lust. I've committed adultery in my heart many times. This is something that God recognizes I will do—and I have done it—and God forgives me for it.

JIMMY CARTER

SINGERS

I'm not going to tell you what's missing in American music.
I never telegraph my moves.

JAMES BROWN

I'm a country songwriter and we write cry-in-your-beer
songs. That's what we do. Something that you can slow
dance to.

WILLIE NELSON

I'd rather be dead than singing "Satisfaction" when I'm 45.

MICK JAGGER

They have a disease of the throat.

RUDOLF BING

You've got to have smelled a lot of mule manure before you
can sing like a hillbilly.

HANK WILLIAMS

I don't sing a song unless I feel it. The song don't tug at my
heart, I pass on it. I have to believe in what I'm doing.

RAY CHARLES

If you think you've hit a false note, sing loud. When in doubt, sing loud.

ROBERT MERRILL

Q: Do you think of yourself primarily as a singer or a poet?
A: Oh, I think of myself more as a song and dance man, y'know.

BOB DYLAN

The thing that influenced me was the way Tommy [Dorsey] played his trombone. . . . It was my idea to make my voice work in the same way as a trombone or violin—not sounding like them, but "playing" the voice like those instruments.

FRANK SINATRA

If the music doesn't say it, how can the words say it for the music?

JOHN COLTRANE

Sleep

Early to rise and early to bed
Makes a man healthy, wealthy and dead.

JAMES THURBER

It was such a lovely day I thought it was a pity to get up.

W. SOMERSET MAUGHAM

The interpretation of dreams is the via regia [royal road] to a knowledge of the unconscious element in our psychic life.

SIGMUND FREUD

Sleep is an excellent way of listening to the opera.

JAMES STEPHENS

A sleeping presence is always a mystery, present and absent at the same time, seemingly peaceful, yet in reality off on wild adventures in strange landscapes.

A. ALVAREZ

As we understand the world, so we interpret our dreams.

LEONARD ROY FRANK

Sleep is the best meditation.

THE DALAI LAMA

Sleep is an eight-hour peep show of infantile erotica.

J. G. BALLARD

The lack of sleep you get with a child in your bed is of a higher quality than the lack of sleep you get in the child's.

BILL COSBY

Laugh and the world laughs with you, snore and you sleep alone.

ANTHONY BURGESS

Society

Hell is other people.

JEAN-PAUL SARTRE

All of us do not have equal talent, but all of us should have an equal opportunity to develop our talent.

JOHN F. KENNEDY

Society broadens the mind; solitude deepens it.

LEONARD ROY FRANK

My definition of a free society is a society where it is safe to be unpopular.

ADLAI E. STEVENSON

A civilized society is one which tolerates eccentricity to the point of doubtful sanity.

ROBERT FROST

About one-fifth of the people are against everything all the time.

ROBERT F. KENNEDY

I've always been interested in people, but I've never liked them.

W. SOMERSET MAUGHAM

Spirituality

I'm an atheist, thank God.

DAVE ALLEN

Physical strength can never permanently withstand the impact of spiritual force.

FRANKLIN D. ROOSEVELT

There's always something to pray for.

AARON NEVILLE

My theology, briefly, is that the universe was dictated but not signed.

CHRISTOPHER MORLEY

God is really only another artist. He invented the giraffe, the elephant, and the cat. He has no real style. He just goes on trying other things.

PABLO PICASSO

God has been replaced, as he has all over the West, with respectability and air conditioning.

AMIRI BARAKA (LEROI JONES)

All inspiration is from a higher power. The body is a shell. The creative spot is from God. I acknowledge that. You hear voices, everybody does. When you get older, you refer to it as intuition.

EDDIE MURPHY

A God who let us prove his existence would be an idol.

DIETRICH BONHOEFFER

Sports

Sports is the only entertainment where, no matter how many times you go back, you never know the ending.

NEIL SIMON

The only thing that's certain is that they'll play the National Anthem before every game.

RICK MONDAY

If you watch a game, it's fun. If you play it, it's recreation. If you work at it, it's golf.

BOB HOPE

I have only one superstition. I make sure I touch all bases when I hit a home run.

BABE RUTH

There are three important things in life: family, religion, and the Green Bay Packers.

VINCE LOMBARDI

Golf is the most fun you can have without taking your clothes off.

CHI CHI RODRIGUEZ

Show me a man who plays a good game of golf, and I'll show you a man who's neglecting something.

JOHN F. KENNEDY

I hate all sports as rapidly as a person who likes sports hates common sense.

H. L. MENCKEN

I'd rather hit than have sex.

REGGIE JACKSON

I never saw a game without taking sides and never want to see one.

WARREN G. HARDING

I believe that professional wrestling is clean and everything else in the world is fixed.

FRANK DEFORD

Next to religion, baseball has furnished a greater impact on American life than any other institution.

HERBERT HOOVER

Football players, like prostitutes, are in the business of ruining their bodies for the pleasure of strangers.

MERLE KESSLER

There's something about football that no other game has. There's sort of a mystique about it. It's a game in which you can feel a clean hatred for your opponent.

RONALD REAGAN

Sports is like a war without the killing.

TED TURNER

Football is violence and cold weather and sex and college rye. Horse racing is animated roulette. Boxing is smokey halls and kidneys battered until they bleed. Tennis and golf are best played, not watched. Basketball, hockey, and track meets are action upon action, climax upon climax, until the onlooker's responses become deadened. Baseball is for the leisurely afternoon of summer and for the unchanging dreams.

ROGER KAHN

The bigger they come, the harder they fall.

BOB FITZSIMMONS

Strategy

An ally has to be watched just like an enemy.

LEON TROTSKY

Make every decision as if you owned the company.

ROBERT TOWNSEND

It is never wise to try to appear to be more clever than you
are. It is sometimes wise to appear slightly less so.

WILLIAM WHITELAW

You can't expect to hit the jackpot if you don't put a few
nickels in the machine.

FLIP WILSON

To choose one's victim, to prepare one's plan minutely, to
stake an implacable vengeance, and then go to bed. . . .
There is nothing sweeter in the world.

JOSEPH STALIN

Trust everybody, but cut the cards.

FINLEY PETER DUNNE

Nature rewards perilous leaps. The prudent atom insists upon its safety now.

W. H. AUDEN

There is no sweeter sound than the crumbling of one's fellow man.

GROUCHO MARX

If people screw me, I screw back in spades.

DONALD TRUMP

Get mad. Then get over it.

COLIN POWELL

Take calculated risks. That is quite different from being rash.

GEORGE S. PATTON

Float like a butterfly, sting like a bee!

MUHAMMAD ALI

When you are skinning your customers, you should leave some skin on to grow so that you can skin them again.

NIKITA KHRUSHCHEV

I never tried to outsmart nobody, it was easier to outdummy them.

DIZZY DEAN

I do unto others what they do unto me, only worse.

JIMMY HOFFA

I never trust a man unless I've got his pecker in my pocket.

LYNDON B. JOHNSON

When you see a rattlesnake poised to strike, you do not wait until he has struck before you crush him.

FRANKLIN D. ROOSELVELT

When the going gets tough, the tough get going.

JOSEPH P. KENNEDY

Forgive your enemies, but never forget their names.

JOHN F. KENNEDY

If you can't convince 'em, confuse 'em.

HARRY S. TRUMAN

STRUGGLE

Struggle does not guarantee success. We have no guarantees, only the knowledge based on the faith of our forebears who did not quit even when they had every reason to do so. Their example is more than our guide. It is our mandate.

DERRICK BELL

To see what is in front of one's nose needs a constant struggle.

GEORGE ORWELL

A revolution is not a bed of roses. A revolution is a struggle to the death between the future and the past.

FIDEL CASTRO

If fate means you to lose, give him a good fight, anyhow.

WILLIAM MCFEE

I will not leave South Africa, nor will I surrender. The struggle is my life. I will continue fighting for freedom until the end of my days.

NELSON MANDELA

Affliction often prepares an ordinary person for an extraordinary destiny.

C. S. LEWIS

Everybody in the ghetto aspires to get out. Nobody with sense wants to live there with rats, roaches, crime and drugs.

ICE-T

Like the course of the heavenly bodies, harmony in national life is a resultant of the struggle between contending forces. In frank expression of conflicting opinion lies the greatest promise of wisdom in governmental action; and in suppression lies ordinarily the greatest peril.

LOUIS D. BRANDEIS

The tougher the fight, the more important the mental attitude.

MICHAEL LANDON

STYLE

Style is knowing who you are, what you want to say, and not giving a damn.

GORE VIDAL

If Botticelli were alive today, he'd be working for *Vogue*.

PETER USTINOV

From the cradle to the coffin underwear comes first.

BERTOLT BRECHT

Haute Couture should be fun, foolish and almost unwearable.

CHRISTIAN LACROIX

"Style" is an expression of individualism mixed with charisma. Fashion is something that comes after style.

JOHN FAIRCHILD

You can be mighty suspicious of a man in boots if he has an indoor complexion.

C. L. SONNICHSEN

All dressed up with nowhere to go.

WILLIAM ALLEN WHITE

Ankles are nearly always good-looking, but knees are nearly always not.

DWIGHT D. EISENHOWER

Style is primarily a matter of instinct.

BILL BLASS

Success

What's money? A man is a success if he gets up in the morning and goes to bed at night, and in between he does what he wants.

BOB DYLAN

The toughest thing about success is that you've got to keep on being a success.

IRVING BERLIN

Success and failure are equally disastrous.

TENNESSEE WILLIAMS

If at first you don't succeed, try, try again. Then quit. No use being a damn fool about it.

W. C. FIELDS

If A equals success, then the formula is A equals X plus Y plus Z, with X being work, Y play, and Z keeping your mouth shut.

ALBERT EINSTEIN

Eighty percent of success is showing up.

WOODY ALLEN

Many a man owes his success to his first wife and his second wife to his success.

JIM BACKUS

To be successful you have to be selfish, or else you never achieve. And once you get to your highest level, then you have to be unselfish. Stay reachable. Stay in touch. Don't isolate.

MICHAEL JORDAN

It never fails: Everybody who really makes it does it by busting his ass.

ALAN ARKIN

If at first you don't succeed, you're about average.

ROBERT ANTHONY

I was born with the restless desire to do a thing as well as it could be done. That meant doing it a little better than the other fellow.

TY COBB

Success is going from failure to failure without loss of enthusiasm.

WINSTON CHURCHILL

Nothing succeeds like a reputation.

JOHN HUSTON

Technology and Progress

That's one small step for a man, one giant leap for mankind.

NEIL ARMSTRONG

Computers are useless. They can only give you answers.

PABLO PICASSO

Our national flower is the concrete cloverleaf.

LEWIS MUMFORD

Progress isn't huge new government programs, it's about making people's lives better little by little.

L. DOUGLAS WILDER

There are three roads to ruin: women, gambling and technicians. The most pleasant is with women, the quickest is with gambling, but the surest is with technicians.

GEORGES POMPIDOU

Technological progress has merely provided us with more efficient means for going backwards.

ALDOUS HUXLEY

The art of our era is not art, but technology. Today Rembrandt is painting automobiles; Shakespeare is writing research reports; Michelangelo is designing more efficient bank lobbies.

HOWARD SPARKS

To err is human but to really foul up requires a computer.

PAUL ERLICH

If it keeps up, man will atrophy all his limbs but the push button finger.

FRANK LLOYD WRIGHT

You can't sit on the lid of progress. If you do, you will be blown to pieces.

HENRY KAISER

The reason that men oppose progress is not that they hate progress but that they love inertia.

ELBERT HUBBARD

Progress in science depends on new techniques, new discoveries and new ideas, probably in that order.

SYDNEY BRENNER

Doonesbury: Excuse me, sir. Do you have any user-friendly sales reps?
Store manager: You mean, consumer compatible liveware? No, he's off today.

GARRY TRUDEAU

If you can't stand the microwaves, get out of the kitchen.

GERALD M. WEINBERG

Technological progress is like an axe in the hands of a pathological criminal.

ALBERT EINSTEIN

Walking in space, man has never looked more puny or more significant.

ALEXANDER CHASE

The automobile changed our dress, manners, social customs, vacation habits, the shape of our cities, consumer purchasing patterns, common tastes, and positions in intercourse.

JOHN KETAS

The machine threatens all achievement.

RAINER MARIA RILKE

Technology is a way of organizing the universe so that man doesn't have to experience it.

MAX FRISCH

Modern technology
owes ecology
an apology.

ALAN M. EDDISON

Progress might have been all right once but it has gone on too long.

OGDEN NASH

Television

I really believe it's a sickness in this country that so many millions of people have nothing better to do than watch a sports event on television.

RED BARBER

Television is more interesting than people. If it were not, we would have people standing in the corners of our rooms.

ALAN CORENK

Television has brought murder back into the home—where it belongs.

ALFRED HITCHCOCK

Television is the first truly democratic culture—the first culture available to everybody and entirely governed by what the people want. The most terrifying thing is what the people do want.

CLIVE BARNES

I find television very educating. Every time somebody turns on the set I go into the other room and read a book.

GROUCHO MARX

Never miss a chance to have sex or appear on television.

GORE VIDAL

Why should people go out and pay to see bad films when they can stay at home and see bad television for free?

SAMUEL GOLDWYN

I invite you to sit down in front of your television set when your station goes on air and stay there without a book, magazine, newspaper, profit-and-loss sheet, or rating book to distract you—and keep your eyes glued to that set until the station signs off. I can assure you that you will observe a vast wasteland.

NEWTON MINOW

Some television programs are so much chewing gum for the eyes.

JOHN MASON BROWN

Cute teenagers exist only on television, I suspect. I know there are none in my neighborhood.

ROBERT MACKENZIE

Television is for appearing on, not looking at.

NOEL COWARD

Television enables you to be entertained in your home by people you wouldn't have in your home.

DAVID FROST

If it weren't for Philo T. Farnsworth, inventor of television, we'd still be eating frozen radio dinners.

JOHNNY CARSON

[Television is] the most powerful tool we can possess in this culture, in this civilization, with which we can address social growth and change.

LEVAR BURTON

It's the medium of entertainment which permits millions of people to listen to the same joke at the same time, and yet remain lonesome.

T. S. ELIOT

THEATER

A talent for drama is not a talent for writing, but is an ability to articulate human relationships.

GORE VIDAL

You can make a killing in the theater, but not a living.

ROBERT ANDERSON

The first rule of the theater—give the best lines to yourself.

ROBERT BLOCH

People want to go to the theatre and go to places where they can see themselves reflected. And if they find that in the theatre that's the place they will go.

LLOYD RICHARDS

This is an industry that doesn't have the common cold. . . . It has cholera.

EMANUEL AZENBERG

[A play:] A snare for the truth of human experience.

TENNESSEE WILLIAMS

The structure of a play is always the story of how the birds came home to roost.

ARTHUR MILLER

It is an extremely difficult thing to put on the stage anything which runs contrary to the opinions of a large body of people.

GEORGE BERNARD SHAW

Drama is life with the dull bits cut out.

ALFRED HITCHCOCK

THINKING AND THOUGHT

"You damn sadist," said mr cummings,
"you try to make people think."

EZRA POUND

Thinking is the activity I love best, and writing is simply thinking through my fingers.

ISAAC ASIMOV

How can I tell what I think until I see what I say?

E. M. FORSTER

A man is but the product of his thoughts; what he thinks, he becomes.

MAHATMA GANDHI

You can't think and hit at the same time.

YOGI BERRA

Tact is the unsaid part of what you think.

WINSTON CHURCHILL

Many people would rather die than think. In fact, they do.

BERTRAND RUSSELL

I do not invent my best thoughts. I find them.

ALDOUS HUXLEY

Change your thoughts, and you change your world.

NORMAN VINCENT PEALE

If I look confused it's because I'm thinking.

SAMUEL GOLDWYN

All modern thought is permeated by the idea of thinking the unthinkable.

MICHEL FOUCAULT

Thinking is the hardest work there is, which is probably the reason why so few engage in it.

HENRY FORD

TRAGEDY

The tragedy of man is what dies inside himself while he still lives.

ALBERT SCHWEITZER

Real tragedy is never resolved. It goes on hopelessly forever.

CHINUA ACHEBE

There are two tragedies in life: one is to lose your heart's desire, the other is to gain it.

GEORGE BERNARD SHAW

A tragic situation exists precisely when virtue does *not* triumph but when it is still felt that man is nobler than the forces which destroy him.

GEORGE ORWELL

The real problem is not why some pious, humble, believing people suffer, but why some do not.

C. S. LEWIS

We are healed of a suffering only by experiencing it to the full.

MARCEL PROUST

I saw the best minds of my generation destroyed by madness, starving hysterical naked.

ALLEN GINSBERG

The tragedy of man is perhaps the only significant thing about him.

EUGENE O'NEILL

Only a great mind overthrown yields tragedy.

JACQUES BARZUN

TRAVEL

I'd rather wake up in the middle of nowhere than in any city on earth.

STEVE MCQUEEN

There are two kinds of travel—first class and with children.

ROBERT BENCHLEY

A man travels the world over in search of what he needs and returns home to find it.

GEORGE MOORE

Airline travel is hours of boredom interrupted by moments of stark terror.

AL BOLISKA

There are two million interesting people in New York and only seventy-eight in Los Angeles.

NEIL SIMON

Travel is glamorous only in retrospect.

PAUL THEROUX

If you look like your passport photo, you're too ill to travel.

WILL KOMMEN

To travel is to discover that everyone is wrong about other countries.

ALDOUS HUXLEY

And that's the wonderful thing about family travel: it provides you with experiences that will remain locked forever in the scar tissue of your mind.

DAVE BARRY

It is easier to find a traveling companion than to get rid of one.

ART BUCHWALD

Unusual travel suggestions are dancing lessons from the gods.

KURT VONNEGUT

Truth

I never give them hell. I just tell the truth and they think it's hell.

HARRY S. TRUMAN

If you're going to tell people the truth, be funny or they'll kill you.

BILLY WILDER

The most awful thing that one can do is to tell the truth. It's all right in my case because I am not taken seriously.

GEORGE BERNARD SHAW

An exaggeration is a truth that has lost its temper.

KAHLIL GIBRAN

The absolute truth is the thing that makes people laugh.

CARL REINER

A great truth is a truth whose opposite is also a great truth.

THOMAS MANN

I have a theory that the truth is never told during the nine-to-five hours.

HUNTER S. THOMPSON

The truth is often a terrible weapon of aggression. It is possible to lie, and even to murder, with the truth.

ALFRED ADLER

Don't lie if you don't have to.

LEO SZILARD

Truth has no special time of its own. Its hour is now-always.

ALBERT SCHWEITZER

I don't want any yes-men around me. I want everyone to tell the truth—even though it costs him his job.

SAMUEL GOLDWYN

Uncomfortable truths travel with difficulty.

PRIMO LEVI

An unexciting truth may be eclipsed by a thrilling lie.

ALDOUS HUXLEY

All truths are half-truths.

ALFRED NORTH WHITEHEAD

Society can only exist on the basis that there is some amount of polished lying and that no one says exactly what he thinks.

YIN YUTANG

It has always been desirable to tell the truth, but seldom if ever necessary.

A. J. BALFOUR

Crushing truths perish by being acknowledged.

ALBERT CAMUS

Truth is what stands the test of experience.

ALBERT EINSTEIN

The United States of America

So this is America. They all seem out of their minds.

RINGO STARR

America is the country where you buy a lifetime supply of aspirin for one dollar, and use it up within two weeks.

JOHN BARRYMORE

Americans never quit.

DOUGLAS MACARTHUR

In America, black *is* a country.

AMIRI BARAKA (LEROI JONES)

The United States is like the guy at the party who gives cocaine to everybody and still nobody likes him.

JIM SAMUELS

America is so vast that almost everything said about it is likely to be true, and the opposite is probably equally true.

JAMES T. FARRELL

What this country needs is dirtier fingernails and cleaner minds.

WILL ROGERS

America . . . just a nation of two hundred million used-car salesmen with all the money we need to buy guns and no qualms about killing anybody else in the world who tries to make us uncomfortable.

HUNTER S. THOMPSON

Ain't nowhere else in the world where you can go from driving a truck to driving a Cadillac overnight. Nowhere.

ELVIS PRESLEY

This is America . . . a brilliant diversity spread like stars, like a thousand points of light in a broad and peaceful sky.

GEORGE BUSH

This will remain the land of the free only so long as it is the home of the brave.

ELMER DAVIS

The fabulous country—the place where miracles not only happen, but where they happen all the time.

THOMAS WOLFE

It was a hard land, and it bred hard men to hard ways.

LOUIS L'AMOUR

There is nothing wrong with America that cannot be cured by what is right with America.

WILLIAM J. CLINTON

The chief business of the American people is business.

CALVIN COOLIDGE

The real death of the United States will come when everyone is just alike.

RALPH ELLISON

UNITY

If we are not our brother's keeper, let us at least not be his executioner.

MARLON BRANDO

It is easier to love humanity as a whole than to love one's neighbor.

ERIC HOFFER

While there is a lower class, I am in it, while there is a criminal element, I am of it; while there is a soul in prison, I am not free.

EUGENE V. DEBS

When Hitler attacked the Jews I was not a Jew, therefore, I was not concerned. And when Hitler attacked the Catholics, I was not a Catholic, and therefore, I was not concerned. And when Hitler attacked the unions and the industrialists, I was not a member of the unions and I was not concerned. Then, Hitler attacked me and the Protestant church—and there was nobody left to be concerned.

MARTIN NIEMOLLER

On this shrunken globe, men can no longer live as strangers.

ADLAI E. STEVENSON

Mankind has become so much one family that we cannot insure our own prosperity except by insuring that of everyone else. If you wish to be happy yourself, you must resign yourself to seeing others also happy.

BERTRAND RUSSELL

Civilization will not last, freedom will not survive, peace will not be kept, unless a very large majority of mankind unite together to defend them and show themselves possessed of a constabulary power before which barbaric and atavistic forces will stand in awe.

WINSTON CHURCHILL

Life is lived in common, but not in community.

MICHAEL HARRINGTON

We live very close together. So, our prime purpose in this life is to help others. And if you can't help them, at least don't hurt them.

THE DALAI LAMA

Violence

Violence solves nothing. Violence always causes more problems than it solves. All violence breeds is pain.

CECIL MURRAY

You can get more with a kind word and a gun than you can with a kind word alone.

JOHNNY CARSON

Returning violence for violence multiplies violence, adding deeper darkness to a night already devoid of stars.

MARTIN LUTHER KING, JR.

Blood alone moves the wheels of history.

BENITO MUSSOLINI

Violence does not and cannot exist by itself; it is invariably intertwined with *the lie*.

ALEKSANDR SOLZHENITSYN

I write about violence as naturally as Jane Austen wrote about manners. Violence shapes and obsesses our society, and if we do not stop being violent we have no future.

EDWARD BOND

Violence is as American as cherry pie.

H. RAP BROWN

Killing cleanly and in a way which gives you esthetic pride and pleasure has always been one of the greatest enjoyments of a part of the human race.

ERNEST HEMINGWAY

Be peaceful, be courteous, obey the law, respect everyone; but if someone puts his hand on you, send him to the cemetery.

MALCOLM X

Today violence is the rhetoric of the period.

JOSÉ ORTEGA Y GASSET

In some cases non-violence requires more militancy than violence.

CESAR CHAVEZ

Our understanding of how to live—live with one another—is still far behind our knowledge of how to destroy one another.

LYNDON B. JOHNSON

War

War is a poor chisel to carve out tomorrows.

MARTIN LUTHER KING, JR.

I believe in compulsory cannibalism. If people were forced to eat what they killed there would be no more war.

ABBIE HOFFMAN

Mankind must put an end to war or war will put an end to mankind.

JOHN F. KENNEDY

Wars of nations are fought to change maps. But wars on poverty are fought to map change.

MUHAMMAD ALI

Usually, when a lot of men get together, it's called war.

MEL BROOKS

War is like love, it always finds a way.

BERTOLT BRECHT

Right is more precious than peace.

WOODROW WILSON

Speaking in terms of evolution, we find that war is not a permanent institution of mankind. If we define war as an instrument of national policy, as an effective way of obtaining the fruits of victory by means of organized force, war has not always been in existence. The chaotic brawls, the internecine fighting of the lowest savages have nothing in common with the institution of war.

BRONISLAW MALINOWSKI

War is war. The only good human being is a dead one.

GEORGE ORWELL

Men love war because it allows them to look serious. Because it is the one thing that stops women laughing at them.

JOHN FOWLES

All wars are popular for the first thirty days.

ARTHUR SCHLESINGER, JR.

I know war as few other men now living know it, and nothing to me is more revolting. I have long advocated its complete abolition, as its very destructiveness on both friend and foe has rendered it useless as a method of settling international disputes.

DOUGLAS MACARTHUR

You can't say civilization don't advance . . . for every war they kill you a new way.

WILL ROGERS

Wars may be fought with weapons, but they are won by men. It is the spirit of men who follow and of the man who leads that gains the victory.

GEORGE S. PATTON

War is to man what maternity is to a woman. From a philosophical and doctrinal viewpoint, I do not believe in perpetual peace.

BENITO MUSSOLINI

Sometime they'll give a war and nobody will come.

CARL SANDBURG

War will exist until that distant day when the conscientious objector enjoys the same reputation and prestige that the warrior does today.

JOHN F. KENNEDY

In war, Resolution; in defeat, Defiance; in victory, Magnanimity.

WINSTON CHURCHILL

Wealth and Poverty

The trouble with being poor is that it takes up all your time.

WILLEM DE KOONING

Don't knock the rich. When was the last time you were hired by somebody poor?

ROBERT ORBEN

When the rich wage war, it is the poor who die.

JEAN-PAUL SARTRE

Let me tell you about the very rich. They are different from you and me. They possess and enjoy early, and it does something to them, makes them soft where we are hard, and cynical where we are trustful.

F. SCOTT FITZGERALD

Will the people in the cheaper seats clap your hands? All the rest of you, if you'll just rattle your jewelry.

JOHN LENNON

I'd like to live like a poor man—only with lots of money.

PABLO PICASSO

Poverty and Suffering are not due to the unequal distribution of goods and resources, but to the unequal distribution of capitalism.

RUSH LIMBAUGH

There were times my pants were so thin that I could sit on a dime and tell if it were heads or tails.

SPENCER TRACY

Poverty—the most deadly and prevalent of all diseases.

EUGENE O'NEILL

It is a matter of having principle. It's easy to have principles when you're rich. The important thing is to have principles when you're poor.

RAY KROC

The great redeeming feature of poverty: the fact that it annihilates the future.

GEORGE ORWELL

I am not rich. I am a poor man with money, which is not the same thing.

GABRIEL GARCÍA MÁRQUEZ

Winning and Losing

Show me a good loser and I will show you a loser.

PAUL NEWMAN

It's not whether you win or lose, it's how you play the game.

GRANTLAND RICE

Someone's always saying, "It's not whether you win or lose," but if you feel that way, you're as good as dead.

JAMES CAAN

You never really lose until you quit trying.

MIKE DITKA

Victory has a hundred fathers, but defeat is an orphan.

JOHN F. KENNEDY

You gotta lose 'em some time. When you do, lose 'em right.

CASEY STENGEL

The important thing is to learn a lesson every time you lose.

JOHN MCENROE

Every time you win, you're reborn; when you lose, you die a little.

GEORGE ALLEN

Victory at all costs, victory in spite of all terror, victory however long and hard the road may be; for without victory there is no survival.

WINSTON CHURCHILL

The victor belongs to the spoils.

F. SCOTT FITZGERALD

Somebody's got to win and somebody's got to lose—I believe in letting the other guy lose.

PETE ROSE

Winning is better than losing.

JOHN F. KENNEDY, JR.

Winning isn't everything, it's the only thing.

RED SANDERS

The problems of victory are more agreeable than those of defeat, but they are no less difficult.

WINSTON CHURCHILL

Witticisms

I smoke cigars because at my age if I don't have something to hang on to, I might fall down.

GEORGE BURNS

Vasectomy means not ever having to say you're sorry.

LARRY ADLER

What is all wisdom save a collection of platitudes?

NORMAN DOUGLAS

Once the toothpaste is out of the tube, it is awfully hard to get back in.

H. R. HALDEMAN

You can't have everything. Where would you put it?

STEVEN WRIGHT

You may certainly not kiss the hand that wrote *Ulysses*. It's done lots of other things as well.

JAMES JOYCE

You can take your choice between God and Sex. If you choose both you're a hypocrite; if neither, you get nothing.

F. SCOTT FITZGERALD

I don't make jokes. I just watch the government and repeat the facts.

WILL ROGERS

What do you give the man who has everything? Penicillin.

JERRY LESTER

Military intelligence is a contradiction in terms.

GROUCHO MARX

I belong to Bridegrooms Anonymous. Whenever I feel like getting married, they send over a lady in a housecoat and hair curlers to burn my toast for me.

DEAN MARTIN

I went on a diet, swore off drinking and heavy eating, and in fourteen days I lost two weeks.

JOE LEWIS

Work

Commuter—one who spends his life
In riding to and from his wife;
A man who shaves and takes a train
And then rides back to shave again.

E. B. WHITE

I get satisfaction of three kinds. One is creating something, one is being paid for it, and one is feeling that I haven't been just sitting on my ass all afternoon.

WILLIAM F. BUCKLEY, JR.

There's no such thing as a free lunch.

MILTON FRIEDMAN

Work is for cowards.

U. J. PUCKETT

The only place where success comes before work is in the dictionary.

VIDAL SASSON

A man's life *is* his work; his work *is* his life.

JACKSON POLLOCK

Work is necessary for man. Man invented the alarm clock.

PABLO PICASSO

Without work, people wither in the soul.

RALPH WILEY

By working faithfully eight hours a day you may eventually get to be a boss and work twelve hours a day.

ROBERT FROST

The better work men do is always under stress and at great personal cost.

WILLIAM CARLOS WILLIAMS

People who work sitting down get paid more than people who work standing up.

OGDEN NASH

Never confuse motion for action.

ERNEST HEMINGWAY

We don't consider manual work as a curse, or a bitter necessity, not even as a means of making a living. We consider it a high human function, as a basis of human life, the most dignified thing in the life of the human being, and which ought to be free, creative. Men ought to be proud of it.

DAVID BEN-GURION

Work is love made visible.

KAHLIL GIBRAN

The brain is a wonderful organ; it starts the minute you get up in the morning and does not stop until you get to the office.

ROBERT FROST

When a great many people are unable to find work, unemployment results.

CALVIN COOLIDGE

The World

A deaf, dumb and blind idiot could have made a better world than this.

TENNESSEE WILLIAMS

The world has narrowed to a neighborhood before it has broadened to a brotherhood.

LYNDON B. JOHNSON

You do not reform a world by ignoring it.

GEORGE BUSH

The world is round. Only one third of its people are asleep at any one time. The other two thirds are awake and causing mischief somewhere.

DEAN RUSK

The world is an oyster but you don't crack it open on a mattress.

ARTHUR MILLER

This is the way the world ends
Not with a bang but a whimper.

T. S. ELIOT

We must learn to live together as brothers or perish together as fools.

MARTIN LUTHER KING, JR.

It's a funny old world—a man's lucky if he gets out of it alive.

W. C. FIELDS

If the world was perfect, it wouldn't be.

YOGI BERRA

I went around the world last year and you want to know something? It hates each other.

EDWARD J. MANNIX

The world is a fine place and worth fighting for.

ERNEST HEMINGWAY

And that's the world in a nutshell—an appropriate receptacle.

STAN DUNN

I think the world is run by C students.

AL MCGUIRE

Writers

I love being a writer. What I can't stand is the paperwork.

PETER DE VRIES

Between the Pulitzer Prize, the American Academy of Arts and Letters, amateur boards of censorship, and the inquisition of earnest literary ladies, every compulsion is put upon writers to become safe, polite, obedient and sterile.

SINCLAIR LEWIS

Every writer creates his own precursors.

JORGE LUIS BORGES

Writing a book is a horrible, exhausting struggle, like a long bout of some painful illness. One would never undertake such a thing if one were not driven on by some demon whom one can neither resist nor understand.

GEORGE ORWELL

The most essential gift for a good writer is a built-in shock-proof shit detector.

ERNEST HEMINGWAY

Many people who want to be writers don't really want to be writers. They want to have been writers. They wish they had a book in print.

JAMES A. MICHENER

Most editors are failed writers—but so are most writers.

T. S. ELIOT

Success comes to a writer, as a rule, so gradually that it is always something of a shock to him to look back and realize the heights to which he has climbed.

P. G. WODEHOUSE

If a writer has to rob his mother, he will not hesitate; the "Ode on a Grecian Urn" is worth any number of old ladies.

WILLIAM FAULKNER

I did not believe political directives could be successfully applied to creative writing . . . not to poetry or fiction, which to be valid had to express as truthfully as possible the individual emotions and reactions of the writer.

LANGSTON HUGHES

Why has the South produced so many good writers? Because we got beat.

WALKER PERCY

Really the writer doesn't want success . . . He knows he has a short span of life, that the day will come when he must pass through the wall of oblivion, and he wants to leave a scratch on that wall—Kilroy was here—that somebody a hundred, or a thousand years later will see.

WILLIAM FAULKNER

It's not a writer's business to hold opinions.

WILLIAM BUTLER YEATS

Writers aren't exactly people . . . they're a whole lot of people trying to be one person.

F. SCOTT FITZGERALD

Good writers define reality; bad ones merely restate it. A good writer turns fact into truth; a bad writer will, more often than not, accomplish the opposite.

EDWARD ALBEE

Never argue with people who buy ink by the gallon.

TOMMY LASORDA

Why do writers write? Because it isn't there.

THOMAS BERGER

Writing

Writing is turning one's worst moments into money.

J. P. DONLEAVY

Writing is a form of self-flagellation.

WILLIAM STYRON

Never talk about what you are going to do until after you have written it.

MARIO PUZO

If you can't annoy somebody, there is little point in writing.

KINGSLEY AMIS

I like to write when I feel spiteful: it's like having a good sneeze.

D. H. LAWRENCE

Forget your personal tragedy. We are all bitched from the start, and you especially have to be hurt like hell before you can write seriously. But when you get the damned hurt, use it—don't cheat with it.

ERNEST HEMINGWAY

In my writing, as much as I could, I tried to find the good, and praise it.

ALEX HALEY

I think a little menace is fine to have in a story. For one thing, it's good for the circulation.

RAYMOND CARVER

There are three rules for writing a novel. Unfortunately, no one knows what they are.

W. SOMERSET MAUGHAM

Novel writing is a highly skilled and laborious trade of which the raw material is every single thing one has ever seen or heard or felt, and one has to go over that vast, smouldering rubbish-heap of experience, half stifled by the fumes and dust, scraping and delving until one finds a few discarded valuables.

EVELYN WAUGH

I always begin with a character or characters, and then try to think up as much action for them as possible.

JOHN IRVING

When in doubt, have two guys come through the door with guns.

RAYMOND CHANDLER

The profession of book-writing makes horse racing seem like a solid, stable business.

JOHN STEINBECK

All of us learn to write in the second grade. Most of us go on to greater things.

BOBBIE KNIGHT

Writing is not a profession but a vocation of unhappiness.

GEORGES SIMENON

No tears in the writer, no tears in the reader. No surprise for the writer, no surprise for the reader. For me the initial delight is in the surprise of remembering something I didn't know I knew.

ROBERT FROST

The tools I need for my work are paper, tobacco, food and a little whiskey.

WILLIAM FAULKNER

Good writing excites me, and makes life worth living.

HAROLD PINTER

Bibliography

8005 Quotes, Speeches & Toasts

Adler, Bill. *The Quotable Conservative.* New York: Carol, 1996.

———. *The Quotable Kennedys.* New York: Avon, 1997.

Andrews, Robert. *Cassell Dictionary of Contemporary Quotations.* London: Cassell, 1996.

Augarde, Tony. *The Oxford Dictionary of Modern Quotations.* Oxford: Oxford University Press, 1991.

Bell, Janet Cheatham. *Famous Black Quotations.* New York: Warner, 1986.

Byrne, Robert. *The 637 Best Things Anybody Ever Said.* New York: Fawcett Crest, 1982.

———. *1,911 Best Things Anybody Ever Said.* New York: Fawcett Columbine, 1988.

Charlton, James. *The Executive's Quotation Book.* New York: St. Martin's Press, 1993.

———. *The Military Quotation Book.* New York: St. Martin's Press, 1990.

Ehrlich, Eugene, and Marshall DeBruhl. *The International Thesaurus of Quotations.* New York: HarperCollins, 1996.

Eigen, Lewis D., and Jonathan P. Siegel, *The Macmillan Dictionary of Political Quotations.* New York: Macmillan, 1993.

Eisen, Armand. *America: Of Thee I Sing.* Kansas City, Missouri: Andrews and McMeel, 1995.

————. *The 1960s: A Book of Quotations*. Kansas City, Missouri: Andrews and McMeel, 1995.

Exley, Helen. *The Best of Father Quotations*. New York: Exley Giftbooks, 1995.

Frank, Leonard Ray. *Influencing Minds: A Reader in Quotations*. Portland, Oregon: Feral House, 1995.

Freeman, Criswell. *The Book of Cowboy Wisdom*. Nashville, Tennessee: Walnut Grove Press, 1997.

Goodman, Ted. *The Forbes Book of Business Quotations: 14,713 Thoughts on the Business of Life*. New York: Black Dog and Leventhal Publishers, 1997.

Grant, George, and Karen Grant. *Letters Home: Sage Advice from Wise Men and Women of the Ages to Their Friends and Loved Ones*. Nashville, Tennessee: Cumberland House, 1997.

Green, Lee. *Sportswit: More Than 1,700 Classic Quotes, Quips and Quick Retorts, Timeless Tales and Anecdotes from and about the World of Sports*. New York: Ballantine Books, 1984.

Gross, David C., and Esther R. Gross. *Jewish Wisdom: A Treasury of Proverbs, Maxims, Aphorisms, Wise Sayings, and Memorable Quotations*. New York: Walker, 1992.

Hale, Helen. *The Art and Artist's Quotation Book: A Literary Companion*. London, Great Britain: Robert Hale, 1988.

Hyman, Robin. *NTC's Dictionary of Quotations*. Lincolnwood, Illinois: National Textbook Company, 1994.

King, Anita. *Contemporary Quotations in Black*. Westport, Connecticut: Greenwood, 1997.

Kipfer, Barbara Ann. *Bartlett's Book of Business Quotations*. New York: Little, Brown, 1994.

Lansky, Bruce. *Age Happens: The Best Quotes & Cartoons about Growing Older*. New York: Simon & Schuster, 1996.

MacHale, Des. *Best Irish Humorous Quotations*. Dublin: Mercier Press, 1997.

Mackay, Alan L. *A Dictionary of Scientific Quotations*. Bristol, England: Institute of Physics Publishing, 1991.

Malloy, Merrit. *Irish-American Funny Quotes*. New York: Sterling, Inc., 1994.

Metcalf, Fred. *The Penguin Dictionary of Modern Humorous Quotations*. New York: Penguin, 1986.

Miner, Margaret, and Hugh Rawson. *American Heritage Dictionary of American Quotations*. New York: Penguin, 1997.

Monges, Suzanne. *Cheer Up! Words of Encouragement*. Kansas City, Missouri: Andrews and McMeel, 1998.

Nathan, David H. *Baseball Quotations*. New York: Ballantine, 1991.

Peter, Dr. Laurence J. *Peter's Quotations: Ideas for Our Time*. New York: Bantam, 1977.

Platt, Suzy. *Respectfully Quoted: A Dictionary of Quotations from the Library of Congress*. Washington, D. C.: Congressional Quarterly, 1992.

Porter, Dahlia, and Gabriel Cervantes. *365 Reflections on Fathers*. Holbrook, Massachusetts: Adams Media Corporation, 1998.

The Princeton Institute. *21st Century Dictionary of Quotations*. New York: Dell, 1993.

Reagan, Michael, and Bob Phillips. *The All-American Quote Book*. Eugene, Oregon: Harvest House, 1995.

Reed, Maxine. *And Baby Makes Three: Wise and Witty Observations on the Joys of Parenthood*. Chicago: Contemporary Books, 1995.

Seldes, George. *The Great Quotations*. Seacaucus, New Jersey: Citadel, 1960.

———. *The Great Thoughts*. New York: Ballantine, 1985.

Shwartz, Ronald B. *The 501 Best and Worst Things Ever Said about Marriage*. New York: Carol, 1995.

Shea, Richard. *The Book of Success*. Nashville: Rutledge Hill Press, 1993.

Simpson, James B. *Simpson's Contemporary Quotations: The Most Notable Quotes Since 1950.* Boston: Houghton Mifflin, 1988.

Vitullo-Martin, Julia, and J. Robert Moskin. *The Executive's Book of Quotations.* Oxford: Oxford University Press, 1994.

INDEX